Collins

175 YEARS OF DICTIONARY PUBLISHING

easy learning Grammar & Punctuation

D1333668

Collins

HarperCollins Publishers
Westerhill Road
Bishopbriggs
Glasgow
G64 2QT
Great Britain

First edition 2009

Reprint 10 9 8 7 6 5 4

© HarperCollins Publishers 2009

ISBN 978-0-00-726921-1

Collins® is a registered trademark of
HarperCollins Publishers Limited

www.collinslanguage.com

A catalogue record for this book is
available from the British Library

Typeset by
Davidson Publishing Solutions, Glasgow

Printed in Italy by
LEGO Spa, Lavis (Trento)

All rights reserved. No part of this
publication may be reproduced, stored
in a retrieval system or transmitted, in
any form or by any means, electronic,
mechanical, photocopying, recording or
otherwise, without the prior permission
of the publisher. This book is sold
subject to the conditions that it shall
not, by way of trade or otherwise, be
lent, re-sold, hired out or otherwise
circulated without the publisher's prior
consent in any form of binding or cover
other than that in which it is published
and without a similar condition
including this condition being imposed
on the subsequent purchaser.

Entered words that we have reason
to believe constitute trademarks have
been designated as such. However,
neither the presence nor absence of
such designation should be regarded
as affecting the legal status of any
trademark.

HarperCollins does not warrant that
www.collinsdictionary.com,
www.collinslanguage.com or any other
website mentioned in this title will be
provided uninterrupted, that any
website will be error free, that defects
will be corrected, or that the website or
the server that makes it available are
free of viruses or bugs. For full terms and
conditions please refer to the site terms
provided on the website.

EDITOR
Penny Hands

FOR THE PUBLISHER
Duncan Black
Lucy Cooper
Elaine Higgleton

Collins Easy Learning Grammar and Punctuation is suitable for everyone who wants to improve their English. Whether you are preparing for exams, need a quick look-up guide to English grammar and punctuation, or you simply want to browse and find out more about the English language and how it works, this book offers you the information you require in a clear and accessible format.

The book begins with a clear outline of the different parts of speech, and goes on to describe their different forms and uses. All the main tenses of English are explained and exemplified, with emphasis on their function in everyday English.

Next, you will find a description of different types of statement and clause, with attention given to structures such as question forms, conditionals, and reported speech. A guide to punctuation gives you clear and up-to-date information on important topics such as the use of the apostrophe, capital letters, and full stops.

Collins' belief in the importance of representing real English remains at the heart of all our descriptions of the language. The Collins corpus is a 4 billion-word database containing up-to-date English language from thousands of different spoken and written sources. These include everyday conversations, formal spoken English, newspapers, fiction, and blogs.

This corpus forms the basis of each grammar item, helping us to make confident and accurate decisions about how English grammar works in today's world. Explanations are fully illustrated with examples which remain close to the corpus, occasionally with small changes made so that they can be as clear and helpful as possible.

Finally, we have used our extensive experience in language teaching and learning to identify typical problems that people experience with English grammar. We draw attention to some of the commonest errors, and give tips to help you avoid them. These include such issues as misuse of the apostrophe, over-use of exclamation marks, and incorrect use of important words.

We hope you enjoy finding out more about this important area of the English language. For more information about Collins language reference books, visit us as www.collinslanguage.com.

6 contents

Grammar

Parts of speech

Sentences are made up of **words**. A sentence can be made up of any number of words.

> *He left us.*
> *The man in the corner lowered his newspaper.*
> *Whenever I see Tammy I worry about how I look.*
> *Until tomorrow then.*
> *Yes.*

We can put words together in many ways to make new sentences.

> *I can help you.*
> *Can I help you?*

Grammar describes how we put words together. Each word in a sentence belongs to a particular set or **class**, depending on how it is used. These classes are called **parts of speech**.

All sentences begin with a capital letter and end in either a full stop, a question mark, or an exclamation mark. When we talk about these marks, e.g. commas, semicolons, full stops, brackets, and so on, we are talking about **punctuation**.

The term **clause** is used to describe a group of words that contains a **verb**, the **subject** of that verb, and, often, some other words such as an **object**.

> *I live in Sussex.*
> *...where I live.*
> *Jessica lived in Manchester at first.*
> *He was living in Rome that year.*
> *...when he had eaten breakfast.*

A sentence can contain one or more **clauses**.

I can help you if you will let me.
Whenever you need to talk to someone, just pop in and see
if I'm here.

Many sentences are made up of a single clause. Single clause sentences are called **simple** sentences.

He arrived on Friday.
My brother loves his skateboard.

A clause always contains a **verb**.

run	*walk*
think	*believe*

A sentence, however, does not always have to be a clause. See p. 258 for more about clauses.

Certainly not.
Until tomorrow then.
Yes.
Why?

A **phrase** is just a **group** of words. The term is usually kept for words which go together naturally.

the other day
my friend Henry
in spite of
over the hill
would have been walking

Many words can refer to one thing only or to more than one. We use the terms **singular** and **plural** for this. A more general term is **number**. Pronouns and nouns can be singular or plural in grammatical number. See p. 200.

When we want to identify the speaker or the person spoken about in grammar, we use **first person** to mean the speaker, **second person** to mean the person who is spoken to, and **third person** to mean the person who is spoken about. For example, we talk about 'first person plural' or 'third person singular'.

pronouns	singular	plural
1st person	I	we
2nd person	you	you
3rd person	he, she, it	they
nouns	the man a girl	the men two girls

A **verb** tells us about an action or a state of being. Ordinary verbs are called **main verbs**.

come	go	think
want	economize	believe

A main verb is sometimes called a 'doing word'. A special group of verbs are called **auxiliary verbs**. These can be put together with main verbs to form different tenses.

> I am thinking.
> She has seen the film already.
> I can help you.
> We might need to.

A **noun** is a word that labels a thing or an idea. Nouns are sometimes called 'naming words'.

table	book	ugliness
time	animal	thing

If we do not want to repeat the same noun in a sentence or a paragraph we can replace it with a **pronoun**. A pronoun is a word that is used instead of a noun phrase or a noun.

> *Gary saw Sue so he asked her to help him.*
> *Ross was hungry so he stopped at a burger bar.*

An **adjective** gives more information about a noun. Adjectives help us describe or pick out which particular thing among many is being referred to. Adjectives are sometimes called 'describing words'.

> *a man*   *a tall man*
> *their TV*   *their new wide-screen TV*
> *the cat*   *the fat black-and-white cat*

A **determiner** is used to point more precisely to the person, thing, or idea that is being talked about. Examples of determiners are **definite** and **indefinite articles** and **possessives**.

> *the cat*   *a man*
> *my aunt*   *their TV*

An **adverb** gives information about the way that an action is carried out or when and where it takes place.

> *She ran quickly down the path.*
> *The children laughed hysterically.*
> *He lifted the box carefully.*

Some adverbs can also be used before adjectives,

> *He was a rather tall man.*
> *This cake is quite nice.*
> *It was fairly good.*
> *It's a very hot day.*

or to introduce a sentence. Many adverbs are formed from adjectives by adding -*ly*.

> *Fortunately, the rain stayed away.*
> *Honestly, I can't help it.*

A **preposition** is one of a small group of words that can be used with nouns and verbs. Prepositions give information about position or movement.

> *on the bridge*   *over the rooftops*
> *in the morning*   *at the gates*

When a preposition is used in front of a noun, the two together do the work of an adverb.

> *He is coming now.*
> *He is coming in the morning.*
> *I found him there.*
> *I found him near the gates.*

A **conjunction** joins two or more nouns or clauses to each other. Conjunctions are sometimes called 'joining words'.

> *I went to the shop and bought some bread.*
> *I bought some bread, but I forgot to get the milk.*

Many words can act as more than one part of speech. It is not unusual for an English word to be a **noun** in one sentence and a **verb** in another sentence.

> *Jamal scored several runs.*
> *She runs half a mile each morning.*
> *I've been chosen for the school play.*
> *Christopher and Angus play golf together on Fridays.*

Parts of the sentence

Sentences consist of a number of parts, using different parts of speech. The most important parts of speech are:

- The **subject**, which is either a noun phrase (see p. 133) or a pronoun (see p. 200). Normally the subject comes before the verb phrase in a sentence.

  > *The girls had been swimming.*
  > *The new teacher came in.*
  > *They had finished.*

- The **verb phrase**, which includes the main verb and which may have auxiliary verbs to go with it. See also pp. 28–87.

  > *The girls had been swimming.*
  > *The new teacher came in.*
  > *They had finished.*
  > *She uses her skateboard quite a lot.*
  > *Rajiv was reading a new novel.*
  > *She is riding someone else's horse.*

- The **object**, which is a noun phrase or a pronoun.

  > *She used her old skateboard.*
  > *Rajiv was reading a new novel.*
  > *Josh found it.*

Not all verbs need an object. When there is one, the object normally comes after the verb phrase. Some verbs may also need an **indirect object**. See also p. 228.

> *Hamish gave* me *a party invitation.*
> *Ruth gave* Lauren *a nice bunch of flowers.*

- An **adverbial**, or **adjunct**, which is an optional part of the sentence.

This may be:

– a single word, an **adverb**.

> *Suddenly, it started to rain heavily.*

– an **adverbial phrase**, a group of words that functions as an adverb.

> *In the morning, the sky was clear.*
> *You probably won't notice it after a while.*

– an **adverbial clause**, a group of words including a verb, which functions as an adverb.

> *I'll get some biscuits for you when I've poured the drinks.*
> *When I've poured the drinks, I'll get some biscuits for you.*
> *Mark played while Isabel sang.*

Though some adverbials have a fixed position, most can be added to a sentence in several places. Any number of them can be added, limited only by the sense of the sentence.

> *In the winter, the roads get very slippery.*
> *The roads get very slippery in the winter.*

- A **complement**. With certain verbs, such as *be* and *seem*, a complement takes the place of an object. A complement can be either an adjective or a noun phrase. Complements provide further descriptive detail about the subject. See also p. 230.

> *He became a doctor in 2005.*
> *Andrew is a motor-mechanic.*
> *He felt a bit silly when he realized what he'd done.*
> *They became good friends despite the mistake.*

Direct and indirect objects

The **object** of a sentence (if there is one) normally comes after the verb phrase. Whether there is an object or not depends on the meaning of the verb. For example, if you want to talk about what someone is doing, you might say *'She is writing'* but if you want to talk about the point of the activity, you might say, *'She is writing a book'*.

> *She was riding.*
> *She was riding her horse.*
> *Erica was writing.*
> *Erica was writing a letter.*

An object that follows a verb like this is called the **direct object**.

> *Rory found a pen.*
> *Our cat doesn't like milk.*

Some verbs also have another sort of object, called an **indirect object**. An indirect object names the person for or to whom something is done. It is usually needed with verbs like *give, find* and *owe*. For example, with *give*, we need to name both the thing that is given and the person it is given to.

> *Mike owes* Tom *five pounds.*
> *Rob gave* me *a box of chocolates.*
> *Susan bought* her rabbit *some more food.*

Some verbs must always take a direct object, some never take a direct object; others sometimes take one and sometimes don't, depending on the meaning. When a verb has an object it is called a **transitive** verb.

> *Rowan bought a magazine.*
> *I don't like rap music.*

When it does not have an object it is called an **intransitive** verb.

> *Lynn fainted.*
> *Patrick screamed.*
> *Soon, everyone was shouting.*

Some verbs may be either **transitive** or **intransitive**.

> *Ann was reading (a letter).*
> *Kim was drawing (a picture).*

When a verb has both an indirect and a direct object it is called a **ditransitive** verb.

> *Amy owes* **Mark** *ten pounds.*
> *Stephen gave* **me** *some flowers.*
> *Katie bought* **her hamster** *a new cage.*

A direct object is needed where the meaning of the verb requires something to give it a focus. This is why we sometimes say that a direct object 'complements' a verb.

- Some verbs must have an adverbial as well as a direct object, for example to specify a place.

> *He placed* **the parcel** *on the chair.*
> *She put* **the umbrella** *in a corner.*

Verbs

Verbs are words that allow us to talk about activities, processes, states of being, and states of mind.

> *This basket holds quite a lot.*
> *John was reading Katherine's essay.*
> *Fiona is preparing a talk for next week's class.*
> *Helen feels much happier now.*
> *I forgot that it was your birthday.*
> *Paul owned several old motorbikes.*

Verbs can be divided into two major groups, according to the way they are used. Those in the larger group are called **main verbs**. The rest are called **auxiliary verbs**.

Verb phrase

A verb phrase can be a single word or a group of associated words.

> *he walks*
> *he is walking*
> *he had walked*
> *he can walk*
> *he has been walking*
> *he might have been walking*

When a verb phrase consists of a single word it is called a **simple** verb. Many verbs in English are made by combining an auxiliary verb and a main verb; this is called a **compound** verb.

- When we want to talk about everything to do with a verb, we use the term **verb phrase**.

Main verbs

These are the verbs that we use to indicate actions and states. Most of the verbs in English are main verbs. They are also called **lexical** verbs. Main verbs are divided or **classified** in several ways:

– according to whether they refer to **states**

> *I can really taste the herbs in this omelette.*
> *This scarf belongs to me.*
> *He hates losing.*
> *She always liked boats and sailing.*
> *I already feel that I have known you for ages.*

or **actions**.

> *Three boys were kicking a ball around in the field.*
> *We were running across the football field.*
> *For six hours, Stuart drove across open desert.*

– into **regular** and **irregular** verbs according to the spelling of their forms.

> *regular: talk, talks, talking, talked.*
> *irregular: swim, swims, swimming, swam, swum.*
> *irregular: go, goes, going, went, gone.*

– according to whether or not they are followed by an object. That is, whether they are **transitive** or **intransitive**. See p. 81.

> *I can read.*
> *We both read the same newspaper.*
> *Don't tell me.*
> *We both ran away.*
> *Sue found a bracelet.*
> *I saw my best friend on Friday.*

Auxiliary verbs

These verbs are used in combination with main verbs in order to allow us to talk about different times or periods of time, different degrees of completion, and different amounts of certainty or doubt. There are several types of auxiliary verb. The **primary** auxiliaries help express time, and the **modal** auxiliaries help to express certainty and doubt. See pp. 35–74.

Tense

We use verbs to talk about actions and states. Verbs **tenses** allow us to talk about the time when the action or state takes place.

All main verbs have two **simple** tenses, the **present simple** and the **past simple**.

present simple	past simple
I walk	I walked
she sings	she sang
they come	they came
you bring	you brought

In these tenses the verb is used on its own without any auxiliary verbs.

English verbs also have **compound** tense forms. In these tenses the main verb is accompanied by one or both of the auxiliary verbs *be* and *have*. See p. 88 for more on tenses.

Aspect

The compound tenses of the verb express two **aspects** – **continuous** and **perfect**.

- The term **aspect** is used to talk about continuing actions versus completed actions or states. Simple tenses do not have aspect.

continuing actions	
I am walking	I was walking
she is singing	she was singing
they are coming	they were coming
you are bringing	you were bringing

completed actions	
I have walked she has sung they have come you have brought	I had walked she had sung they had come you had brought

We use these compound verbs when we want to talk about:

– the continuous nature of an action (using a form of the auxiliary *be + -ing*). This is called the **continuous aspect**.

> *I am still studying French.*
> *He was living in London all that year.*
> *James is helping out with the children this week.*
> *Sara and Scott were looking for a new flat at the time.*

– the completion of an action (using a form of the auxiliary *have* + a past participle, usually *-ed*). This is called the **perfect aspect**.

> *I have been a teacher for four years.*
> *He had lived in London for a year before coming to Sussex.*
> *James has helped out before.*
> *Sara and Scott had found their flat by then.*

The two aspects of the verb can be joined so that we can talk about the duration and the completion of an action in the same verb phrase. See pp. 88–89 for more on tense and aspect.

> *I have been studying French for four years.*
> *I had been living in London for four years when I met him.*
> *James has been helping us this week.*

Simple tenses

Simple tenses show moments in time, timeless states, and habitual or repetitive actions.

> It *tastes* good.
> Julie *keeps* a diary.
> Adrian *went* home at midnight.
> She *heard* a strange noise in the night.
> Rob usually *walks* to school.
> Yesterday he *went* by car.

The **present simple** and the **past simple** of regular verbs are formed by using the base form of the verb. See pp. 94–97.

Continuous tenses

Continuous tenses show duration or continuity.

> It *is raining* hard this morning.
> It *was raining* when we came out of school yesterday.
> I'm *having* dinner. Can I call you back?
> He *was listening* to the radio when he heard the news.

The **present continuous** and the **past continuous** are formed from either the present or the past tense of the verb *be* + the **present participle** (or '-*ing* form') of the main verb. See pp. 98–101.

Perfect tenses

The present perfect tense shows that an action is completed but that it still has some importance in the present time.

> Ken *has walked* all the way from the station. (...and he's tired.)
> He *has never visited* me. (...and I'm feeling neglected.)
> She *has missed* the train. (That's why she's not here.)

The **past perfect** is used to talk about something that happened in a time before a particular time in the past.

> He told us that he *had tried* it before.
> I *had never been* climbing before our activity holiday last year.
> She was late because she *had missed* her train.

The **present perfect** and the **past perfect** are formed using either the present or the past tense of the verb *have* + **the past participle** of the main verb. See pp. 102–105.

Perfect continuous tenses

Perfect continuous tenses show duration, completion, and importance in the present time.

> I *have been working* hard in the garden all day.
> My mother *has been helping* me.
> My sisters *have been riding* all day.
> I *had been working* in Italy that summer.
> Some of us *had been waiting* for two hours when the
>   doctor appeared.

The **present perfect continuous** and the **past perfect continuous** are formed using either the present or past tense of the verb *have* + **the past participle** of *be* + **the present participle** of the main verb. See p. 106.

Other verb forms

Other verb combinations are used for positive or negative statements, or to express degrees of time and probability.

> *Do you like espresso coffee?*
> *I don't like fried food.*
> *Could I have a coke, please?*
> *You will be in Edinburgh within two hours.*
> *They will probably meet us at the station.*

Types of main verb

Verbs of action

Most verbs describe an action such as *walking*, *running*, or *reading*.

> *John is running for the train.*
> *Sophie has just bought a new camera.*
> *She is putting on an exhibition of her photographs.*
> *Robbie has seen the film already.*

When we need a verb to describe a new activity, we can either invent a new word, or we can adapt other parts of speech.

> *You can use your phone to access the internet.*

• Action verbs can be expressed in all the tenses.

Verbs of state

Some verbs are used to talk about states of being or states of mind.

These include:

– verbs relating to the senses, e.g. *feel, hear, see, smell, taste*
– verbs relating to emotions, e.g. *adore, fear, hate, like, love, want, wish*
– verbs relating to mental activity, e.g. *agree, believe, expect, forget, mean*
– verbs relating to possession, e.g. *belong, own, possess*

> *I feel unhappy.*
> *I hate arguments.*
> *These flowers smell gorgeous.*
> *Rob wishes he hadn't agreed to the plan.*
> *We mean you no harm.*
> *That car belonged to us once.*

- Verbs of state are not usually used in continuous tenses. When they are used in continuous tenses, they change their meaning.

  > *I'm just feeling to see if the bone is broken.*
  > *We were tasting some interesting New Zealand wines.*
  > *Naomi is expecting a baby.*

There are some uses of the verb *be* that allow you to choose between a state or an action meaning. The word used as the complement makes an important difference.

  > *Mark is being silly*   but not *Mark is being tall.*
  > *Oscar is being nasty*   but not *Oscar is being intelligent.*

The verb *seem* has a limited number of adjectives that can be used as its complement.

  > *Simon seems happy*   but not *Simon seems tall.*

The forms of main verbs

English verbs have up to five different forms. These are:

1 the base form, e.g. *pull*
2 the 3rd person singular,
   present simple tense, e.g. *pulls*
3 the past simple tense, e.g. *pulled*
4 the past participle, e.g. *pulled*
5 the present participle, e.g. *pulling*

- Regular verbs are all formed in the same way, by building on the **base form** (form 1). This is the form you normally find in a dictionary. Most verbs are regular.

- Irregular verbs have different forms, particularly forms 3 and 4. See p. 32.

Form 1: The **present simple** tense has all but one of its forms the same as the **base form**.

Form 2: When the **present simple** tense has a 3rd person singular subject, the verb is formed from the **base form** + -*s*.

Form 3: The **past simple** is formed from the **base form** + -*ed*.

Form 4: The **past participle** is formed from the **base form** + -*ed*.

Form 5: The **present participle** is formed from the **base form** + -*ing*.

A special variation of the base form is the *to* **infinitive**. There are a number of uses of a verb where both the words *to* + the **base form** must be present.

The base form is sometimes called the 'bare infinitive'.

As mentioned above, the 3rd person singular is formed from the **base form + -s**. Below are the exceptions to the rule:

Verbs ending in **-o**, **-ch**, **-sh**, **-ss**, **-x**, **-z** or **-zz**: add **-es** to make the 3rd person singular, e.g.

torpedo	he torpedo**es**
catch	he catch**es**
focus	he focus**es**
push	he push**es**
miss	he miss**es**
box	he box**es**
buzz	it buzz**es**

Verbs ending in **-y** after a consonant: change **y** to **i** and add **-es**, e.g.

carry	he carr**ies**
fly	he fl**ies**
worry	he worr**ies**

As mentioned above, the present participle is made up of the **base form + -ing**. There are some exceptions to the rule. All verbs that contain a short final vowel in front of a final consonant double the consonant before -ing, e.g.

sob	sobbing
bid	bidding
flog	flogging
run	running
stop	stopping
get	getting
put	putting

Irregular verbs

Irregular verbs are verbs that *do not* form the past simple tense and the past participle by adding *-ed* to the base form.

The three main groups of irregular verbs

In Group A, the base form, the past simple and the past participle are the same:

1 the base form	*put*
2 the present simple tense	*puts*
3 the past simple tense	*put*
4 the present participle	*putting*
5 the past participle	*put*

A	*bet*	*cut*	*let*	*set*	*spread*
	burst	*hit*	*put*	*shed*	*thrust*
	cast	*hurt*	*shut*	*split*	*upset*

In Group B, the past simple and the past participle have the same form:

1 the base form	*buy*
2 the present simple tense	*buys*
3 the past simple tense	*bought*
4 the present participle	*buying*
5 the past participle	*bought*

B1

base form	past form	base form	past form
bend	bent	hang	hung
bind	bound	have	had
bleed	bled	hear	heard
bring	brought	keep	kept
build	built	kneel	knelt
buy	bought	lay	laid
catch	caught	make	made
find	found	say	said

Some of these verbs have alternative spellings for the past participle:

B2 The past form may be either *a* or *b*.

base form	past forms		base form	past forms	
burn	burnt	burned	smell	smelt	smelled
dream	dreamt	dreamed	spell	spelt	spelled
lean	leant	leaned	spill	spilt	spilled
learn	learnt	learned	spoil	spoilt	spoiled

In Group C, the base form, the past simple, and the past participle all have different forms:

1	the base form	go
2	the present simple tense	goes
3	the past simple tense	went
4	the present participle	going
5	the past participle	gone

C

base form	past forms		base form	past forms	
arise	arose	arisen	ring	rang	rung
awake	awoke	awoken	rise	rose	risen
bear	bore	borne	saw	sawed	sawn
begin	began	begun	see	saw	seen
bite	bit	bitten	shake	shook	shaken
blow	blew	blown	show	showed	shown
break	broke	broken	shrink	shrank	shrunk
fly	flew	flown	strive	strove	striven
give	gave	given	take	took	taken
know	knew	known	throw	threw	thrown
ride	rode	ridden	write	wrote	written

Auxiliary verbs

An auxiliary verb is a verb that is used together with a main verb to show time and continuity.

- *Be* and *have* are the **primary auxiliaries**. A primary auxiliary is used to construct compound tenses.

- *Be* is used to make present continuous and past continuous tenses

> *I am working.*
> *Rob is using the computer.*
> *We were all wondering about that.*
> *Kevin was teaching in America in 1985.*

and also for the passive. See p. 40 for more on *be*.

> *These books are sold in supermarkets.*
> *Martin was arrested and held overnight.*

- *Have* is used to make present perfect and past perfect tenses. See p. 44 for more on *have*.

> *Stephen has finished fixing the car.*
> *George and Alice have seen the show already.*
> *Amanda had already eaten when we arrived.*
> *They had not expected to see us there.*

- *Do* is the **supporting auxiliary**. It is used in forming negatives, questions, and emphatic statements. See p. 48 for more on *do*. See pp. 88–93 for more on simple and compound verb forms.

> *I do not like sausages at all.*
> *Do you like prawns?*
> *You do like prawns, don't you?*

- *Will*, *may*, *might*, and the other verbs listed on pp. 53–54 are the **modal auxiliary verbs**, usually called simply, **modal verbs**. A modal verb allows us to talk about actions as possible, doubtful, or necessary.

    > *Charlie will go home on Friday.*
    > *Charlie may go home on Friday.*
    > *Charlie could go home on Friday.*
    > *Charlie must go home on Friday.*

Auxiliaries can be combined together in a single verb phrase. For example, a verb phrase may consist of a **modal** + a form of *have* + a form of *be* + a form of a **main verb**.

> *I could have been making a bad mistake by trusting him.*
> *Sara will have been living in New Zealand for 2 years*
>   *next month.*
> *You must have been given the wrong number.*

The auxiliary verb, or if there is more than one of them, the first auxiliary verb, performs these following grammatical functions:

– It shows **tense** and is the **finite** part of the verb phrase.

> *I have seen it.*
> *She had seen it.*
> *She has been thinking.*
> *She had been thinking.*

– It shows **number** and **person** agreement with the subject.

> *She has seen it.*
> *They have seen it.*
> *I am looking for it.*
> *You are looking for it.*

– It will take any **negative** immediately after it.

> *I do not want to do that.*
> *She has not been concentrating.*

– It can come before the subject to make a **question**.

> *Do you want to help us?*
> *Have you got a mobile phone?*

Contracted forms

Auxiliaries are very often used in contracted forms. In the case of *be* and *have*, the contracted form can involve linking the subject and the auxiliary verb into a single form e.g. *I'm, I've, we'd, Sue's (Sue has or Sue is)*.

> *We're back!*
> *(We are back!)*
> *I've found it.*
> *(I have found it.)*
> *They'd gone when I got there.*
> *(They had gone when I got there.)*
> *Tom's here.*
> *(Tom is here.)*

The contracted negative form **auxiliary** + *n't* is common with all the auxiliaries except *am*, e.g. *hasn't, wouldn't, don't*.

> *She isn't (is not) trying.*
> *We don't (do not) live here.*
> *He hasn't (has not) seen it.*
> *I can't (cannot) come.*

In standard British English, the contracted form of *am not*, when it is part of a question, is *aren't I*.

> *Aren't I going to need some matches?*
> *I'm getting a lift with you, aren't I?*

- Contracted forms are more informal than full forms. They are therefore more common in spoken English. Full forms are usually preferred in formal written English.

Auxiliaries are used in sentence tags. See p. 241 for more about sentence tags.

> *You had only just bought that carpet when the kitchen flooded, hadn't you?*
> *It's Katie's birthday on Saturday, isn't it?*
> *You are joking, aren't you?*

Auxiliaries are also used to make a short addition to a statement, such as:

- a positive addition to a positive statement, accompanied by *so* or *too*.

> *I went to the park and Lucy did too.*
> *I loved the film, and so did Finlay.*

- a negative addition to a negative statement, accompanied by *neither* or *nor*.

> *My dad never eats mussels and neither do I.*
> *I don't want to speak to William now. – Nor do I.*
> *I can't understand it. – Neither can I.*

- Auxiliaries can be used in positive sentences to give emphasis. When they are emphatic they are never contracted.

  You have made a mess!
  That was a nice surprise!
  I am proud of Katie. She's so clever.

In the present simple tense and the past simple tenses the appropriate form of *do* is used to show emphasis.

  I do like Penny. – So do I.
  We did have a lovely time.

An auxiliary on its own can be used to give a short answer to a question. Whatever auxiliary is used in the question is used on its own in the answer. The main verb is not repeated. Short answers are very common in spoken English.

  Do you like avocados? Yes, I do. or *No, I don't.*
  Have you read anything by Michael Morpurgo?
    Yes, I have.

Be

The verb *be* is used as an auxiliary verb and it can also be used as a main verb. See p. 28.

The verb *be* is irregular. It has eight different forms: *be*, *am*, *is*, *are*, *was*, *were*, *being*, *been*. The present simple and past simple tenses make more changes than those of other verbs.

I am late.	*We are late.*
You are late.	*You are late.*
He is late.	*They are late.*

I was late.	*We were late.*
You were late.	*You were late.*
She was late.	*They were late.*

The present participle is *being*.

> *He is being very helpful these days.*

The past participle is *been*.

> *We have been ready for an hour.*

- The present simple tense forms of *be* are often contracted in normal speech. Note that the contracted form of *they are* is spelled *they're*, and not *their* which is the possessive form of *they*.

I'm here.	*We're here.*
You're here.	*You're here.*
He's here.	*They're here.*

Any form of *be* is made negative by adding *not* immediately after it. In speech, some forms of *be* also have contracted negative forms. Some of these forms emphasize the negative.

	emphasizes the negative
I'm not late.	
You aren't late.	You're not late.
He isn't late.	He's not late.
We aren't late.	We're not late.
They aren't late.	They're not late.
I wasn't late.	
You weren't late.	
He wasn't late.	
We weren't late.	
They weren't late.	

The major uses of *be* as an auxiliary verb are to form continuous tenses and the passive.

- **Continuous** tenses of main verbs use the appropriate form of *be*, present or past, followed by the present participle (or *-ing* form). See p. 98 and p. 106.

- The **passive** form of a main verb uses the appropriate form of *be* followed by the past participle. See p. 118.

The verb *be* is also used as a main verb. It is commonly found joining a subject to its complement.

As a **main verb**, *be* is used to talk about:

- Feelings and states. For this we use the simple tenses of the verb with a suitable adjective. See p. 88.

    I am delighted with the news but he is not happy.
    She was busy so she was not able to see me.

- People's behaviour. For this we use the continuous tenses of the verb with a suitable adjective. See p. 96.

  > *I am not being slow, I am being careful.*
  > *You were being very rude to your mum when I came downstairs.*

- *Be* + the *to* **infinitive** is sometimes used to refer to future time. This is a rather formal use, which often appears in news reports. See pp. 128–132.

  > *The Prime Minister is to visit Hungary in October.*
  > *The Archbishop is to have talks with the Pope next month.*

- *It + be*: we use *it* as a subject when we are talking about time, distance, weather, or cost. In this use, *be* is always singular.

  > *Hurry up, it's eight thirty!*
  > *Is it? I didn't know it was so late.*

  > *It's thirty miles to Glasgow.*
  > *Come and visit us. It's not very far.*

  > *It's cold today but it isn't wet.*

  > *It's very expensive to live in London.*

- *There + is/are* is used to talk about something existing. In this use, the form that *be* takes may be singular or plural, depending on the number of the noun, and *be* is sometimes contracted.

  > *There's a spare toothbrush in the cupboard.*
  > *There was a cold wind blowing.*
  > *There isn't enough petrol for the journey.*
  > *There are several petrol stations on the way, aren't there?*

To make the continuous tenses of the main verb *be* we have to use *be* twice, once as an auxiliary and once as a main verb.

> *You are being so annoying!*
> *I know I am being silly, but I am frightened.*

The question form of clauses with the verb *be* in them is made by putting the appropriate form of *be* right in front of the subject.

> *Are you better now?*
> *Is he free this morning?*
> *Was he cooking dinner when you arrived?*

Have

The verb *have* is used as an auxiliary verb

> *She has run a lovely, deep, bubble bath.*
> *Katie had read about the concert in the newspaper.*

and also as a main verb. See p. 24.

> *She is having a bath at the moment.*
> *The driver has had his breakfast, so we can go.*

The verb *have* has the forms: *have, has, having, had*. The base form of the verb is *have*. The present participle is *having*. The past tense and past participle form is *had*.

- The present and past forms are often contracted in everyday speech, especially when *have* is being used as an auxiliary verb.

  The contracted forms are:

have = **'ve**	*I've seen the Queen.*
has = **'s**	*He's gone on holiday.*
	Ian's behaved badly.
had = **'d**	*You'd better go home.*
	Ian'd left them behind.

The form *have* contracts to *'ve*. This can sound rather like *of*, especially after other auxiliary verbs.

> *She would've given you something to eat.*
> *You could've stayed the night with us.*
> *If he'd asked, I might've lent him my car.*

Avoid the common mistake of writing *of* in this case.

As an **auxiliary** verb, *have* is used to make the **perfect tenses** of main verbs.

The **perfect** tenses of main verbs use the appropriate form of *have*, present or past, followed by the past participle. See pp. 102–109.

> *I have read some really good books over the holidays.*
> *I had seen the film before.*

The negative of a clause containing a compound verb with *have* is made by adding *not* or another negative word immediately after the appropriate form of *have*. In speech, some forms of *have* also have contracted negative forms.

> *I have never seen such luxury.*
> *Rachel had not been abroad before.*
> *She had hardly had time to eat when Paul arrived.*

- present tense and past tense forms that emphasize the negative element:

I/we/you/they've not;   *he/she/it's not*
I/we/you/he/she/it /they'd not

> *She's not told me about it yet.*
> *We've not been here before.*
> *They'd not seen him for weeks.*

- present tense and past tense negative forms that are used less emphatically:

I/we/you/they haven't;   *he/she/it hasn't*
I/we/you/he/she/it /they hadn't

> *He hasn't found anywhere to stay this holiday.*
> *We haven't been here before.*
> *They hadn't looked very hard, in my opinion.*

As a **main verb**, *have* is used to talk about:

- states or conditions, such as possession or relationship.

- In these uses, continuous tenses are not possible. With this meaning *have* is sometimes used alone, adding only *not* to make negatives, and adding nothing to make questions.

    > *I have something for you.*
    > *We haven't anything for you today.*
    > *Have you no sense of shame?*
    > *The driver has had his breakfast, so we can go.*
    > *We had a good time.*

    It is also often used with forms of *do* to make negatives and questions.

    > *Do you have a pen?*
    > *Does she have my umbrella?*
    > *She doesn't have any brothers or sisters.*
    > *Do you have time to see me now?*

- *Have got* is an informal form of this main verb use of *have*, often used in speaking, especially in British English.

    > *I haven't got any brothers or sisters.*
    > *Has she got my umbrella? – Yes, she has.*
    > *She hasn't got any money.*

- activities, including those such as eating, and leisure.

With this meaning of *have*, negatives and questions are formed using one of the forms of *do*.

> *He was having a shower when I phoned.*

I'm having lunch at twelve o'clock.
Come and have a sandwich with me,
No thanks. I don't usually have lunch.

He's having a day off.
Did you have a good holiday?

Contractions and weak forms are not possible with this meaning.

Have got is not used with this meaning.

* to express obligation using *have to* or *have got to*.

I've got to go now, I'm afraid.
Do you have to leave so soon?
Have you got to leave so soon?

> When *have* is a main verb, it makes perfect forms like all
> other main verbs. This means that it is possible to use
> *have* twice in present or past perfect sentences, once as
> an auxiliary verb and once as a main verb.
>
> *We have had enough, thank you.*
> *They had already had several warnings.*

Do

The verb *do* is used as an auxiliary verb.

> *I do not want it.*   *We do not want it.*
> *You do not want it.*   *You do not want it.*
> *He does not want it.*   *They do not want it.*

> *I did not want it.*   *We did not want it.*
> *You did not want it.*   *You did not want it.*
> *She did not want it.*   *They did not want it.*

It can also be used as a main verb. See p. 28. When *do* is used as an auxiliary verb it is a **supporting verb**. Because a main verb cannot combine directly with negatives or make questions, *do* is used to support the main verb.

> *Don't talk!*
> *Don't run!*

It is also used to stand in for another verb to avoid repetition, as shown on p. 39.

The verb *do* is irregular. It has five different forms: *do*, *does*, *doing*, *did*, *done*. The base form of the verb is *do*. The past simple form, *did*, is the same throughout. The present participle is *doing*. The past participle is *done*.

The present simple tense *do* and the past simple tense *did* can be used as an auxiliary verb. As an auxiliary, *do* is not used with **modal** verbs.

> *I do not want it.*   *We do not want it.*
> *You do not want it.*   *You do not want it.*
> *He does not want it.*   *They do not want it.*

I **did** not want it.	We **did** not want it.
You **did** not want it.	You **did** not want it.
She **did** not want it.	They **did** not want it.

As an **auxiliary** verb *do* is used in the following ways:

- to help make the negative and question forms of present simple and past simple tenses.

    *Oh dear, I **didn't feed** the cat this morning.*
    ***Do** you **know** what time it is?*
    ***Did** Tim **pay** for his ticket last night?*

- to make the negative form of a command.

    ***Don't** talk!*
    ***Don't** run!*

- to make a command more persuasive. See p. 246.

    ***Do** let me see it!*

- to avoid repeating a main verb in additions, commands, sentence tags, and short answers.

    *They often go to the cinema, **and so do** we.*

    *Don't run on the road! Don't **do** it!*

    *You live in Glasgow, **don't** you?*

    *Do you play cricket? – No, I **don't**.*
    *Did they tell you the news? – Yes, they **did**.*
    *Jim likes jazz, I think. Yes, **he does**.*

- in comparisons.

> *She sings better than I do.*

The positive forms of *do* cannot be contracted. In speech, the negative has contracted forms.

> *I don't (do not) agree with you.*
> *She doesn't (does not) live here now.*
> *They didn't (did not) buy any food.*

- present tense negative forms:
  I/we/you/they don't; he/she/it doesn't

- past tense negative form:
  I/we/you/he/she/it/they didn't

When *do* is a main verb, it has a range of meanings that includes *carry out*, *perform*, *fix*, or *provide*. It is sometimes used in place of a more specific verb.

> *I'll do the lawn now.*
> *(I'll mow the lawn now.)*
> *I'll do you.*
> *(I'll punch you.)*
> *We don't do coach parties.*
> *(We don't serve coach parties.)*

It is then used with the full range of tenses and forms. See also p. 94.

> *Are you doing your homework?*
> *You have been doing well this term.*
> *She had done enough, so she stopped.*
> *This has been done before.*

The main verb use of *do* can be used to talk about:

– habits.

> *I do the washing up every evening.*
> *This what I usually do.*

– behaviour.

> *He did something rather foolish.*
> *I didn't do anything wrong.*
> *What are you doing?*

– plans.

> *What are you doing on Sunday?*

As a main verb, *do* makes negatives and questions like all other main verbs:

– in the present simple tense with auxiliary *do*.

> *What does he do for a living?*
> *Do I do it this way?*
> *No, you don't do it like that at all.*

– in the past simple tense with auxiliary *did*.

> *Did Henry do it, then?*
> *Didn't Henry do it, then?*
> *He didn't do it, you know.*

This means that it is possible to use *do* twice in negative and interrogative sentences; once as an auxiliary verb and once as a main verb.

- As a main verb, *do* can be used with modal verbs.

  *They **will do** it for you, if you ask nicely.*
  *I **can do** it, but I **shouldn't do** it.*

Modal verbs

Modal verbs are a particular kind of **auxiliary**.

> *Look, I can do it! – Oh yes! So you can.*
> *Can I use your phone? – Of course you can.*
> *Do you think she will come? – I'm sure she will.*
> *I must get our tickets today.*

Modal verbs are used when you need to add special elements of meaning to a main verb, e.g.:

- to express different degrees of doubt and possibility about the action of the main verb.

  > *I may not be able to do it.*
  > *I think that I might have caught your cold.*
  > *I could ask for you, if you like.*
  > *You couldn't do it, could you?*

- to express degrees of future possibility, ranging from the definite future, *will*, to the possible future, *may*, and the conditional future, *could*.

  > *You will be seeing her on Friday at Jackie's house.*
  > *I may be late home tomorrow evening.*
  > *I could bring some more bread home with me tonight.*

- to request or give permission for an action to take place.

  > *May I come in?*
  > *You can borrow my car tonight if you like.*

- to make a prohibition, when used with a negative.

  > *You shouldn't use this computer without permission.*
  > *You cannot borrow my car tonight.*
  > *He must not see this letter.*

– to speculate.

> *The weather's so bad the flight could be late.*
> *It might be all over by the time we get there.*
> *He may be very cross about all this.*

– to express obligation and duty.

> *I must give in my essay today.*
> *Helen ought to tell the truth.*

– to refer to typical behaviour.

> *She can be very kind on occasions like this.*

– to add politeness to a request which might otherwise sound abrupt.

> *Would you please close the door.*

– to make conditional sentences (see p. 273).

– in reported speech (see p. 279).

Modals can refer to a time range that reaches from the immediate present to some future time, so that they can all be used for future reference, especially when they are used with a time adverbial. See pp. 110–117.

> *You will be seeing her on Friday at Jackie's house.*
> *I may be late home tomorrow evening.*
> *I could bring some more bread home with me tonight.*

Some modals can refer to a time range that goes back from the immediate present to some indefinite past time. They can refer to habitual action when they are used with a time adverbial.

> *When I was little, I would ride my bike round and round the lawn.*

Form

Unlike other verbs, modal verbs have only one form, the **base form**, and only one tense, the present simple.

> *You will be seeing her on Friday at Jackie's house.*
> *I may be late home tomorrow evening.*
> *I might go to visit Grandma on Saturday.*

They do not have a *to* infinitive. They have no *-s* inflection in the 3rd person singular.

> *He will be seeing her on Friday.*
> *She may be late home.*

- Since modal verbs do not have past tense forms, you have to use other verbs to provide some of the modal meanings in the past, e.g. past necessity is expressed by *had to* instead of *must*.

> *I must visit Auntie May today.*
> *I had to visit Auntie May yesterday.*

- The modals *shall* and *will* are usually contracted to *'ll* in spoken English. All the negative forms can be contracted to form a single word such as *can't*, *won't*, *wouldn't*. These contracted forms are common in both spoken and written English.

> *I will/shall = I'll*
> *We will/shall = we'll*
> *You mustn't say things like that, Jane.*
> *John can't come to my party.*

There are other contracted forms such as *he'll*, *we'll*, *shan't*, and *they'll*, which are common in spoken English but rare in written English.

- Several verbs act as modals sometimes and as full main verbs at other times. These are called **semi-modal verbs**.

   How dare he!
   He dared to ask me to do his washing!
   She needn't come if that's how she feels.
   Monica needs a new raincoat.

Position

Modals come before any other auxiliary verb or main verb in the verb phrase.

- Modal verbs are followed by the **base form** of the verb if there is no other auxiliary verb present.

   Yes, you can borrow those earrings tonight.
   You should try that new restaurant in town.
   You must come over again some time.

If one of the auxiliary verbs *have* or *be* follows the modal verb, the main verb will take the appropriate present or past participle form.

   I may have upset him.
   You could have looked for it yourself.
   Janice might be coming too.
   Sue will have been worried about her, I imagine.

- In negative sentences, *not* comes immediately after the modal verb and in front of all the other verbs.

   They may not wait for you if you're late.
   He must not be disturbed after 9 o'clock.

- *Can* cannot be combined with the auxiliary form *have*, but the negative form *can't* can be combined with *have*.

    *They **can't have seen** him.*   **but not** *They can have seen him.*

Can and could

Both these verbs indicate ability in some respect. The use of *could* is usual in clauses that contain a reference to past time.

> *Morag can speak French quite well now.*
> *I couldn't play chess two years ago, but I can now.*

> *When I was younger I could play tennis really well.*
> *Winston is so strong he can lift me right off my feet.*
> *Can you get up the stairs without help?*
> *You can come over for dinner whenever you like.*

Can and *could* are used:

– to indicate that you know how to do something.

> *Mary can do these sums.*
> *I couldn't draw very well when I was younger.*

– to show ability to do something. (Compared with *be able to*, *can* indicates ability of a more general nature that includes 'is permitted to'.)

> *When I was younger I could ski really well.*
> *Graham can run ten miles in 25 minutes.*
> *Are you able to walk to the car?*

– to make polite requests or to ask for permission:

Could is more tentative than *can*. (Compare with *may*, which is more formal.)

> *Can I borrow the car tomorrow evening, Mum?*
> *Could I come with you on the trip?*
> *May I take this book home with me?*

- to express the possibility of an action in the future, especially when the possibility is related to plans or projects. (Compare with *may*, where the possibility referred to is still uncertain and in the future.)

> *We can go to Paris next week since you are free.*
> *We could go to Paris next week if you are free.*
> *We may go to Paris, but it depends on our finances.*

- to express the possibility of an action in the present.

> *You can dive off these rocks; it is quite safe here.*
> *We could dive off the rocks, but we must take care.*

- to talk about actions that were possible but did not happen, using *could* + the perfect form of *have*.

> *Mary could have stopped the fight but she didn't.*

- using the perfect form of *have*, to speculate about actions that have recently taken place.

> *Who could/can have broken the window?*
> *Who would have guessed that they were related?*

A distinction between *can* and *could* is observed in conditionals. *Could* is used when the conditions are not met.

> *If Louisa is coming, she can look after the children for a while.*
> *If Helen had more money, she could buy a computer.*

When changing sentences from direct to reported speech *can* is usually changed to *could*.

> *Bernard said, 'I can do it for you, Sue.'*
> *Bernard said that he could do it for Sue.*

can

The negative form is:　　　　　　　　　*cannot*.

> *I **cannot** understand why he did it.*

The contracted negative form is:　　*can't*.

> *I **can't** help it.*

could

The contracted negative form is:　　*couldn't*.

> *I **couldn't** help it.*

May and might

Both *may* and *might* can be used in requests and in expressions of possibility for the present and future.

> *Might I ask you your name?*

> *The weather **may/might** be better tomorrow.*
> *Craig **may/might** know his results soon.*
> *We **may/might** go to the cinema tonight.*

> *'**May** I come with you?' Nicky asked.*
> *Nicky asked if she **could** come with them.*

May and *might* are used as follows:

– *May* is used to ask permission in a more formal way than *can*.

> ***May** I have a drink, please?*
> ***May** I use your ruler? I've lost mine.*

Might is occasionally used in formal situations.

> ***Might** I suggest a different solution?*

– *May* is used to give permission, particularly when applied to *you, he, she, they* or a proper noun, to show that the speaker is allowing something to happen.

> *You **may** go now.*
> *Users **may** download forms from this website.*

– Both *may* and *might* are used to express the possibility of some future action; *might* is more tentative than *may*.

> *The weather **may/might** be better tomorrow.*
> *Craig **may/might** know his results soon.*
> *We **may/might** go to the cinema tonight.*

- *May* is often used for politeness, to make an order appear as a request; *might* is used to make the speaker more remote from the request.

    You might give that idea a bit more consideration.
    You might want to move a bit closer to the screen.

- *Might* is occasionally used when someone is trying to persuade another person to do something, perhaps with some degree of irritation. This use is a little old-fashioned.

    You might give me some cake too, Lucy.
    Anna, come on, you might tell me what he said!

• When *might* is used in a conditional sentence, the *if* clause can be in the present or the past tense. Compare with *could*. See p. 58.

    If Louisa comes, she might look after the children.
    If Louisa came, she might look after the children.

When changing sentences from direct to reported speech *may* usually becomes *could*.

    'May I come with you?' Nicky asked.
    Nicky asked if she could come with them.

may
The contracted negative form is: none or *mayn't* (rare).

might
The contracted negative form is: *mightn't*.

    He mightn't have enough money.
    We might come and live here, mightn't we, mum?

Must

Must is used to express obligation, give orders and give advice. It can only be used for present and future reference. When the past is involved, you use *have to*.

Must is used:

– to express obligation.

> *All pupils must bring a packed lunch tomorrow.*

– to give orders firmly and positively.

> *You must go to sleep now.*

– to give advice or make recommendations emphatically.

> *You must get one of these new smoothie-makers – they're great!*
> *You must see 'Nim's Island' – it's brilliant.*

– to speculate about the truth of something.

> *She must be mad!*
> *You must be joking!*
> *There must be some mistake.*
> *Mr Robertson is here; it must be Tuesday.*

When this sort of statement is made in the negative or interrogative, *can* is used instead.

> *Can Mary be joking? Can she really mean that?*
> *You can't be serious!*
> *It can't be true!*

- *Must* can be used in the interrogative, but many speakers prefer *have to* instead.

    > *Must you go so soon?*
    > *Must I invite Helen?*
    > *Do you have to go soon?*
    > *Do I have to invite Helen?*

You can use *must* with a negative:

- to forbid someone to do something.

    > *You must not cross when the light is red.*
    > *You must not say things like that.*

- to talk about an event or state that is unacceptable.

    > *There mustn't be any mistakes in your letter.*
    > *The whale must not become extinct.*

> Note that to express the fact that you are not obliged to do something, you use *do not have to*.
>
> Compare:
>
> > *You must not come in here.*
> > *You don't have to come in here (if you don't want to).*

- It is necessary to change *must* to *have to* when changing sentences from direct to reported speech.

    > *'I must fill out those forms this evening,'* said Ian.
    > *Ian said that he had to fill out some forms.*

must

The contracted negative form is: *mustn't*.

> You **mustn't** *worry so much.*

Shall and will

The normal way to express simple future time in English is using the modal verb *will* followed by the **base form** of a main verb.

> The modal verb *shall* is not used very much in modern English, except in suggestions or offers of help.
>
> *Shall I help you? Shall I cook supper?*
> *Shall we go to the cinema tonight?*

Any distinction between *will* and *shall* is difficult to make in spoken English, since the contracted form, *'ll*, is used to mean both *shall* and *will*.

Shall is used:

– with questions involving *I* and *we* when the speaker is making a suggestion or offering help.

> *Shall I help you? Shall I cook supper?*
> *Shall we go to the cinema tonight?*

Will is used:

– with *I* and *we* to show intentions and to make promises.

> *Don't worry. I shan't/won't be late and Helen won't be late either.*
> *We shall/will be in touch.*
> *I shall/will try to ensure that you get a good room.*

– with *you*, *he*, *she*, *it*, and *they*, to give reassurances.

> *He will be well treated.*
> *You will have your money next week.*

– to insist on something. Full forms are normally used, and are stressed in speech.

> *You will do what I tell you!*
> *Jane will go to Mary's even if I have to carry her there.*

– to make polite requests and to give invitations.

> *Will you help me look for my purse?*
> *Will you come to lunch on Friday?*

– to give orders.

> *You will finish your work before you watch TV, won't you?*
> *Louisa, will you please be quiet!*

– to show that someone persists in doing something (full form with stress).

> *Oh! Tony will keep jogging me when I'm trying to write!*
> *No wonder you feel sick. You will eat chocolate all day long.*

– to show prediction.

> *The match will be finished by now.*
> *I think it will probably rain tomorrow.*

will
The contracted form is: *'ll.*

> *He'll be home soon.*

The contracted negative form is: *won't.*

> *Eve won't speak to Harriet.*

shall

The contracted form is: *'ll*.

The contracted negative form is: *shan't* (used mainly in British English).

> I *shan't* *say a word.*

Should

The modal verb *should* is used in the following ways:

– to talk about moral obligation. Compare *ought to* on p. 73.

> *They **should** do what you suggest.*
> *People **should** report this sort of thing to the police.*
> *She suggested we **should** visit Aunty Irene more often.*
> *Rob insisted that we **should** think of others before*
> *ourselves.*

– to give advice or instructions.

> *You **should** undo the top screws first.*
> *You **should** keep your credit card separate from your chequebook.*

– to suggest that something follows on logically from what has just been said.

> *They left here at 6 o'clock, so they **should** be home now.*

– to show politeness in a conditional clause. This use is used in formal written communication.

> *If you **should** decide to go, please contact us.*
> ***Should** you need more information, please call the manager.*

• *Should* can be used with the main verb after certain set expressions such as, *it is a pity that, it is odd that, I am sorry/surprised that*. This is a more formal use than the same expression without *should*.

> *It's a pity that this **should** happen.*
> *I was quite surprised that he **should** be doing a job like that.*

- *Should* + the perfect form of the main verb can be used to express regret about something that was done or not done. Compare with *ought to*.

  > *He should have stopped at the red light.*
  > *You should have told me you were ill.*

- When changing sentences from direct to reported speech, *should* does not change.

  > *Anna said that I should try to relax more.*

In formal English, *should* can be used with *I* or *we* in conditional clauses, instead of the more common *would*. This form is usually, but not always, found together with an **if** clause.

  > *I should love to visit Peru if I had the money.*
  > *I should be very cross if they didn't give me a certificate.*
  > *We should hate to miss the play.*

In this sense, *would* is more common in modern spoken English.

  > *I would love to visit Peru.*
  > *I would be very cross if they didn't give me a certificate.*
  > *We would hate to miss the play.*

should
The contracted negative form is: *shouldn't*.

Would

The modal verb *would* is commonly used as follows:

− to make a polite request.

> *Would you mind moving your bag?*
> *Would you give me a hand with this ladder, please?*

− to offer something politely.

> *Would you like some tea or coffee?*

− together with *like* as a polite form of *want*.

> *We would like to see Mr Brown now, please.*
> *My friends would like to see your garden.*

− to refer to habitual activity in the past, with the meaning of *used to*.

> *I remember Jeff; he would watch TV all day if you let him.*
> *Jess was a kind girl; she would always go out of her way to help people.*

− to show that someone persisted in an activity in the past: *would* is sometimes stressed here.

> *John would keep nagging at her, though I asked him not to.*
> *She would go on and on until I lost my temper.*

− to express and ask about probability.

> *I saw a girl at the window. Who would that be?*
> *Oh, that would be his elder sister!*

– in conditional clauses, usually together with an **if** clause.

> *I would have taken it if it had been available.*
> *If you offered me some more I wouldn't refuse.*
> *Brian would have phoned the police if it he'd seen the accident.*

When changing sentences from direct speech to reported speech, *will* is usually changed to *would*.

> *Anna said, 'Raymond will help you.'*
> *Anna said that Raymond would help us.*
> *James said, 'The car won't start!'*
> *James said that the car wouldn't start.*

would
The contracted form is: *'d.*

> *I'd have done it too, given the chance.*
> *We'd like to look at the garden.*
> *He'd be very angry if he knew about it.*

The contracted negative form is: *wouldn't.*

> *Even if he'd known about it, he wouldn't have been angry.*

Ought to

The use of *ought to* is similar to *should*, but it is much less frequent.

Like *should*, the verb *ought to* does not have a past form. It is only used with reference to the present and the future.

Ought to is rarely used in questions and negatives. When it is, it is confined mainly to formal styles.

In negatives, *not* comes between *ought* and *to*. In questions, the subject comes between *ought* and *to*.

> *I ought not to have said those things to her.*
> *Ought we to make such a sacrifice for the benefit of future generations?*

Ought to is used as follows:

– to express an obligation or an expectation that someone should do something.

> *You ought to listen carefully.*
> *We ought to leave now.*
> *Lucy ought to go by herself.*
> *People ought to be a bit nicer to us.*

– to express the likelihood of something happening.

> *Annabel ought to be here by now.*
> *The journey ought to take about 2 hours.*

– *Ought to + have +* **past participle of main verb** is used to express regret that something was not done or to reproach someone for doing or not doing something.

I ought to have spoken up earlier. I'm sorry.
You ought to have offered to help.
They ought to have told us what to expect.

- In questions and negatives, *should* is frequently used instead of *ought to* because it sounds more natural.

    Ought I to report it to someone in authority?
    Should I report it to someone in authority?
    Ought we to make a start?
    Should we make a start?

ought to
The contracted negative form is: *oughtn't (to)*.

    Oh dear, we oughtn't to have let that happen.
    Well then she ought to do something about it, oughtn't she?

Dare and need

The two verbs *dare* and *need* have characteristics of both modal verbs and main verbs. Because of this, they are called **semi-modals**. They sometimes behave like modal verbs and do not add -s to the form that goes with *he*, *she*, and *it*. That is, they have no 3rd person singular inflection. They are then followed by the **base form** of a main verb.

> *Need I say more?*
> *Dare I ask how the project's going?*

The past form *needed* is not used as a modal; *dared* is occasionally used as a modal.

The modal uses of these verbs are all **negatives** or **questions**.

> *Where will you all be today? – Need you ask?*
> *You needn't come if you're busy.*
> *Dare I suggest that we have a rota system?*
> *I daren't tell him the truth; he'll go crazy.*

Questions that are formed are often set expressions such as *Need I/you ask?*, *Dare I suggest...?* and *Need I/we say more?*

Dare and *need* sometimes behave like main verbs with -s inflection. In this case they are followed by the *to* infinitive. They can also use the auxiliary *do* and have the whole range of tenses appropriate to a main verb.

> *Louisa doesn't need to know.*
> *Does Paul need to go now?*
> *Paul needs to go.*
> *Dare to be different!*
> *I don't dare to mention it to him.*

When *dare* or *need* are used as modal verbs in a positive **statement**, there must be a word of negative meaning in the same clause. This word can be outside the verb phrase and may be a word with a negative sense, such as *only, never, hardly*.

> *He need only ask and I will tell him.*
> *No sensible driver dare risk that chance.*

As a modal verb, *dare* has forms as follows:

I *dare* not *go*.   I *dared* not *go*.
He *dare* not *go*.   He *dared* not *go*.

Dare I *do* it?
Dare he *do* it?
Daren't he *do* it?

As a main verb, *dare* has forms as follows:

I *dare to do* it.   I *do* not *dare to do* it.
He *dares to do* it.   He *did* not *dare to do* it.
He *does* not *dare to do* it.   *Does* he *dare to do* it?
He *doesn't dare to do* it.   *Doesn't* he *dare to do* it?

As a modal verb, *need* has forms as follows:

I *need* not *go*.   *Need* I *go*?
He *need* not *go*.   *Need* he *go*?
He *needn't* go.   *Needn't* he *go*?

As a main verb, *need* has forms as follows:

I *need* it.   I *need to do* it.
He *needs* it.   He *needs to do* it.
I *do* not *need to go*.   I *do* not *need to do* it.
He *does* not *need to go*.   *Does* he *need to go*?

- Either of the two forms of *dare* and *need* can be used for sentences that have much the same meaning.

  *Anna **didn't dare to jump** off the high fence.*
  *Anna **dared not jump** off the high fence.*
  *You **don't need to come** if you don't want to.*
  *You **needn't come** if you don't want to.*

Used to

The verb *used to* is a 'marginal' modal verb. Unlike the other modal verbs, it is only found in the past tense. Therefore, when it is used with *do* to make negatives and questions, the form of the auxiliary verb is always *did*.

Used to is used as follows:

– to describe an activity or a state that happened many times in the past.

> *Gerry always used to go for a run before breakfast.*
> *Peter didn't use to say things like that when I knew him.*

– to refer to an activity or state that was true in the past but is no longer true.

> *I used to like rock climbing when I was younger.*
> *You didn't use to be so stressed!*

Used to takes the following forms:

– The form *used to* is used with all subjects e.g. *I, we, you, he, she, it, they.*

I used to	*We used to*
You used to	*You used to*
She used to	*They used to*

> *I used to live in New Zealand.*
> *He used to deliver newspapers papers but he owns the*
>   *shop now.*
> *Nancy and Bill used to live in California.*

There are two forms for a negative:

– *did not/didn't use to.*

> *We didn't use to have central heating when I was a child.*
> *Alan didn't use to like children, but it's different now he has his own.*

– *used not to.*

> *I used not to be able to watch myself on TV at all.*
> *We used not to worry much about money.*
> *Things usedn't to be so bad.*

There are two forms for a question:

– *did* + **subject** + *use to* + **base form**:
e.g. *did he use to…?*

> *Did they use to visit you often? – Well, Mary used to.*

– *used* + **subject** + *to* + **base form**:
e.g. *used he to… ?*

> *Used he to play the guitar?*

• In negatives, the form with *did* is used the most. In questions, the form with *did* is almost always preferred.

The common contracted negative form is *didn't use to*. The rarer contracted negative form is *usedn't to*.

Do not confuse *used to* + **base form** with *be used to* + **present participle**, where *used to* means *accustomed to*.

> They lived in India for a long time, so they **are used to eating** spicy food.

Phrasal verbs

A **phrasal verb** is a type of verb that is created when a main verb is combined with either:

– an **adverb**,

take off	*give in*
blow up	*break in*

– a **preposition**,

get at (someone)	*pick on (weaker children)*

– or an **adverb** + **preposition**,

put up with (insults)	*get out of (doing something)*

Type A. Verb plus adverb

Some Type A phrasal verbs have no object, i.e. they are **intransitive**. The sentence makes sense without any further addition to the verb.

> *Mary went away.*
> *Helen sat down.*
> *The students came back.*

Others do require an object, i.e. they are **transitive**.

> *We could make out a figure in the distance.*
> *He tried to blow up the Houses of Parliament.*
> *Could you put your clothes away, please?*

If the object is a **noun**, many Type A phrasal verbs will allow the adverb to come either:

– before the object,

> *I picked up* Jim *on my way home.*
> *He blew out* the candle.
> *She tidied away* her things.

– or after the object.

> *I picked* Jim *up on my way home.*
> *He blew* the candle *out.*
> *She tidied* her things *away.*

If the object is a **pronoun**, it must come before the adverb.

> *I picked* him *up.*
> *He blew* it *out.*
> *She tidied* them *away.*

Sometimes you can guess the meaning of these verbs from the meanings of the parts.

> *to sit down* = sit + down
> *to go away* = go + away

Sometimes you have to learn the new meanings, or use a dictionary.

> *to make up (an answer)*   = *invent*
> *to turn down (an invitation)* = *decline*
> *to work out (a problem)*   = *solve*
> *to put up (a visitor)*   = *accommodate*

Type B. Verb plus preposition

Type B phrasal verbs always have an object. This is because prepositions always have an object.

> *He asked for* his bill.
> *He asked for* it.
> *She listened to* the doctor.
> *She listened to* her.
> *They referred to* our conversation.
> *They referred to* it.

Sometimes there are two objects – the object of the verb and the object of the preposition.

> *He asked* the waiter *for* the bill.

Type C. Verb plus adverb and preposition

Type C phrasal verbs are a combination of the two previous kinds of verb. All the parts of a Type C phrasal verb come before the object.

> *We are looking forward to* our holiday/it.
> *Don't put up with* bad behaviour/it.
> *You must look out for* the warning signs/them.

• It is sometimes hard to tell adverbs and prepositions apart, because often the same word can be both a preposition and an adverb, depending on how it is used. For further information about prepositions see p. 219.

The following are examples of the three types of phrasal verb that are explained on p. 81.

Type A

Phrasal verbs made from a verb plus an adverb may be intransitive (do not take an object) or transitive (take an object).

some phrasal verbs that do not take an object	*some phrasal verbs that do take an object*
to break down	to blow something up
to carry on	to break something off
to fall down	to bring a child up
to get about	to bring a subject up
to get up	to catch somebody up
to give up	to clear something up
to go away	to close something down
to go off	to give something up
to go on	to leave something out
to grow up	to make something up
to hold on	to pick someone up

Type B

Phrasal verbs made from a verb plus a preposition are all transitive.

to add to something	to hope for something
to agree with someone	to insist on something
to apply for a job	to laugh at something
to approve of something	to listen to something
to arrive at a place	to look after someone
to ask for something	to look for something
to believe in something	to look into something
to belong to someone	to pay for something
to call on someone	to refer to something
to care for someone	to rely on someone
to come across something	to run into someone
to deal with something	to run over something

Some Type B verbs are doubly transitive, since both the verb and the preposition can have an object.

to **add** insult **to** injury
to **ask** a grown-up **for** help
to **check** your answers **with** the teacher
to **pay** the assistant **for** your shopping
to **refer** a customer **to** the manager

Type C

Phrasal verbs with an adverb plus a preposition all take a prepositional object.

to be fed up with something	to keep away from something
to carry on with something	to look back on something
to catch up with something	to look forward to something
to check up on something	to look out for something
to come up with something	to look up to someone
to cut down on something	to make up for something
to do away with something	to put in for something
to face up to something	to run away with something
to fall back on something	to run out of something
to get on with someone	to run up against something
to get out of something	to stand up for something
to go back on something	to walk out on someone
to go in for something	to watch out for something
to break in on someone	to lead up to something

Tense

Time reference

Verb forms help us make time reference through their **tense**. Tense shows whether an action or a state took place in the past or takes place in the present.

> Jessica works in the post office.
> Laurence worked in the post office over the Christmas
>   holidays.

There are two **simple tenses** and six **compound tenses**.

Simple tenses

The simple tenses consist of a single word.

There is a **present simple** tense

I like	I live
you like	you live
he likes	he lives

and a **past simple** tense.

I liked	I lived
you liked	you lived
he liked	he lived

The simple tenses of regular verbs

The **present tense** is the same as the **base form** of the verb, except that an -s is added to the verb when it has a noun or he, she, or it as a subject. This is called the 3rd person singular form.

> he/she/it likes
> he/she/it lives

The **past tense** of a regular verb is made from the **base form** of the verb with -ed (or -d if the verb already ends in -e) added. The spelling is the same for all persons.

> I liked   I lived
> you liked   you lived
> he liked   he lived

The simple tenses of irregular verbs

Most irregular verbs make the **present tense** from the **base form** of the verb just as regular verbs do.

> Present
> I find   I go
> you find   you go
> he/she/it finds he/she/it goes

- Irregular verbs make the **past tense** in a number of different ways. Sometimes the past tense is a completely different word. See pp. 32–34 for more on irregular verbs.

> Past
> I found   I went
> you found   you went
> he/she/it found he/she/it went

Aspect

When we use a verb, we often need to be able to refer to more than the time at which an event took place. We sometimes need to be able to refer to actions and states as completed or not completed. **Aspect** describes the way we think of verbal actions.

The **continuous aspect** is formed by using the appropriate form of the auxiliary *be* together with the *-ing* form (**present participle**) of the main verb.

We use **continuous aspect** to show that an action:

– is going on at the time of speaking.

> I'm *having* dinner at the moment. Can I call you back?
> I know what you *are doing*!
> Look! Someone's *walking* around in our garden!

– was going on throughout the time that you are referring to.

> I *was having* dinner when he called.
> I *was waiting* for her when she came out of the classroom.
> We *were driving* home when we saw the accident.

– will be going on at the time that you are referring to.

> We're *going* to Turkey for a holiday next year.
> They're *coming* to us for Christmas this year.

The **perfect aspect** is formed by using the appropriate form of the auxiliary *have* together with the *-ed* form (**past participle**) of the main verb.

We use **perfect aspect** to show that an action:

– is complete at the time of speaking.

> *I've finished the book. It was brilliant.*
> *We've enjoyed having you all to stay.*
> *Jo has borrowed the book, so I can't check now, I'm afraid.*

– was complete at the time you are referring to.

> *Oh dear; I had forgotten my promise to Aunt Jane.*
> *Sharon had lost her key, so she had to wait outside.*
> *Sue had seen the film three times already, but she didn't mind.*

It is possible to have a compound tense that shows both aspects, continuous and perfect.

> *Peter has been talking about you a lot recently.*

Compound tenses

The compound tenses are a combination of present or past **tense** (shown through an auxiliary verb) with continuous or perfect **aspect**. See also pp. 88–89.

> I'm *doing* my homework at the moment, so I can't come out.
> Ben *has seen* the camera that he wants.

> She *was listening* to the radio in the kitchen.
> Sandra *had invited* all her friends.

- The tense of the auxiliary verb shows whether the compound verb is **present** tense,

> I'm *having* dinner at the moment; I'll call you back.
> We've *had* a lovely stay; thank you.

or **past** tense.

> We *were dancing* around the living room and singing along.
> Mum *had gone out* and left us some snacks.

The choice of the **auxiliary** and the **participle** shows what aspect the verb has.

– if it is the auxiliary *be* and the *-ing* participle (the present participle), the aspect is **continuous**.

> My brother *is having* a party tomorrow.
> The kids *were running* wild when we got home.

– if it is the auxiliary *have* and the *-ed* participle (the past participle) the aspect is **perfect**.

Jill has walked more than 500 miles for charity.
Someone had tied up the dog to stop it wandering off.

These are the main compound tenses:

present continuous   = present of *be* + *-ing* participle.

    Kerry is waiting until Jessica gets here.

past continuous   = past of *be* + *-ing* participle.

    Maria was watching TV when Jo called.

present perfect   = present of *have* + *-ed* participle.

    Sam has seen a few things that he'd like.
    We've bought some better equipment.

past perfect   = past of *have* + *-ed* participle.

    She had really believed their story!
    Rory had had enough of their silly questions.

A compound verb can also combine both the continuous and perfect aspects, using **two auxiliary verbs** and a **main verb**. This produces the following combinations:

present perfect continuous
    = present of *have* + past participle of *be* + *-ing* participle.

    For the past two months, Zoe has been visiting us once a week.
    We've been trying to finish that job since Easter.

past perfect continuous

= past of *have* + past participle of *be* + *-ing* participle.

> Vicky **had been hoping** for better news.
> I **had been travelling** all day, so I was exhausted.

The modal auxiliaries can be used in compound tenses.

> She **might be babysitting** for us on Friday.
> We **would be sitting** here for hours if I told you everything.
> I **may have eaten** something that disagreed with me.
> I expect Nayeema will **have bought** something for tea.

They come in first position in the verb phrase, so they are followed by:

– the subject and the rest of the verb in questions.

> Will **you be going** shopping after work?

– the negative *not* and the rest of the verb in negative statements.

> Marcus **may not have been** entirely truthful.

– the subject, the negative *not*, and the rest of the verb in negative questions.

> Will **you not be pushing** for that to be changed?

If the contracted negative form of the modal is used, then it comes before the subject and and the rest of the verb.

> Won't he **be calling** on us this evening?

> Modals are not used with the supporting auxiliary verb *do*.

See pp. 58–80 for the meanings and uses of modal auxiliary verbs.

Responses

You usually use just the first part of the verb phrase in a compound verb as the response form. That is, you use one of the auxiliary verbs. If it is a simple tense you use the supporting auxiliary *do*.

> *Do you like avocados? – Yes, I do.*

If one of the forms of *be* or *have* is the first verb in the verb phrase, then use that as the response form.

> *Has Claire been round yet? – Yes, she has.*
> *Was Nayeema asking for help? – Yes, she was.*

If a **modal** verb is first in the verb phrase, some speakers prefer to use the modal and the auxiliary form together as the response form.

> *Do you think he might have left the parcel somewhere? –*
> *Yes, he might or Yes, he might have.*
> *So Laurence could be coming with us then. – Yes, he could*
> *or Yes, he could be.*

The present simple tense

Typical forms of this tense are as in:

>*I know her.*
>*He knows her.*

The present simple tense of *do* is used as the supporting auxiliary when you want to:

− ask a question,

>*Do I know you?*
>*Does she know you?*

− make a negative statement using *not*,

>*I do not know her.*
>*She does not know you.*

− or give a short response.

>*Do you just have coffee for breakfast? – Yes, I do.*

We use the present simple tense to talk about:

− habits, likes and dislikes, and things that happen regularly.

>*I like coffee for breakfast but everyone else in my family*
>   *prefers tea.*
>*I don't take sugar in my coffee.*
>*What does Jamie usually have for breakfast?*
>*They often go to the cinema on Saturdays.*
>*I don't usually watch TV.*

(When we talk about habits, we often add adverbs such as *often*, *always*, *usually*, *sometimes*, or *never*, or adverbial phrases such as *on Sundays* or *in the summer*.)

- statements of fact that are scientific truths or that are about a permanent state.

> *The sun rises in the east.*
> *Birds fly south in the winter.*
> *We live in Scotland.*

- statements that indicate the speaker's opinions or beliefs.

> *I think he's a very good teacher.*
> *I don't agree with that at all.*

- for dramatic narrative to tell a story or describe an action vividly,

> *He walks slowly to the checkout and puts his bag on the counter. As the cashier opens the till he draws a gun ...*

- or when giving a commentary on a sports event or public function.

> *... but Nadal sees it. He runs up to the net and smashes the ball.*

We can also use the present simple for planned future actions with a time adverb, for example to talk about travel plans and timetables. See pp. 110–117 for more about future reference.

> *The train leaves at 10.40 a.m. and arrives at 3.30 p.m.*

We use the present simple in conditional sentences about real possibilities that affect the future. See p. 273 for more on conditional sentences.

> *If I lend you my notes, I won't be able to revise tonight.*

The past simple tense

Typical forms of this tense are as in:

> I *met* her.
> She *met* him.
> I *went* there.
> She *went* there.

Because the past simple consists of one word only, the past simple tense of *do*, which is *did*, is used as the supporting auxiliary when you want to:

– ask a question,

> *Did* I *meet* him?
> *Did* she *meet* him?
> *Did* I *go* there?
> *Did* it *go* there?

– make a negative statement using *not*,

> I *did* not *meet* her.
> He *did* not *meet* her.
> I *did* not *go* there.
> He *did* not *go* there.

– or make a response.

> *Did you see Jenny yesterday?* – No, I *didn't*.
> *Did Penny phone you ?* – Yes, she *did*.

We use the past simple tense to talk about:

− single actions in the past.

> He **locked** the door and **left** the house.
> I **went** out and **brought** the cat back in again.

− habitual actions in the past, often with *always*, *never*, or *often*.

> In those days I **always went** to Juliano's for lunch.
> I **cycled** in **every day** and that soon **made** me fit.
> I **often visited** Glasgow on business when I was in publishing.

− past actions where a definite time is mentioned. It is often used with a time expression such as *ago* or *last month*, when the action is seen as finished.

> **Some time ago** now, I **went** to America for a month.
> **Once upon a time** there was a king in a faraway land.
> I **saw** Roger **a little while back**.
> I **bought** the microwave **a year ago**.

− points where the main action is broken. The rest of the sentence uses the past continuous tense to describe the past activity or action.

> I was clearing out the garage when a car **came** down the drive.
> We were leaving the house when the phone **rang**.

The present continuous tense

Typical forms of this tense are as in:

>*I am winning.*
>*He is winning.*

>*Am I winning?*
>*Is she winning?*

>*I am not winning.*
>*He is not winning.*

>*Aren't I winning?*
>*Isn't she winning?*

>*Am I not winning?*
>*Is she not winning?*

Some main verbs are not normally used in the continuous in standard British English, though they may be used this way in other varieties of English. These are generally verbs about states rather than actions.

>*I am winning.*   but not *I am liking it.*
>*I am not winning.*   but not *I am not liking it.*

We use the present continuous tense to talk about:

– things that are happening now, at the time when we are talking.

>*Mum's mowing the lawn, and I'm doing my homework,*
>   *but Isabel isn't doing anything.*
>*The children aren't asleep; they're messing about.*
>*Come on; you're not trying.*

When you give a short answer to a question, it is normal to echo the auxiliary but not the main verb.

> *Are you waiting for someone? – Yes, I am.*
> *Is Hamish working in the library? – No, he isn't.*

– a temporary activity, even if it is not happening at the time when we are talking.

> *I'm studying German at college.*
> *I'm thinking of getting a new car.*

– a temporary situation in contrast to a permanent situation.

> *I'm living in Scotland at the moment.*
> *Fiona is working in the stables over the holidays.*

– a changing state or situation.

> *My headache is getting better.*
> *The daylight is slowly fading.*

– the circumstances under which something is generally done.

> *I have to wear glasses when I'm driving.*

– arrangements for future events along with a time adverb or phrase. See p. 110 for more on the future.

> *I am flying to New York next week.*

We also use it to express annoyance at a repeated action. In this case, one of the following adverbs is used with the verb: *always, forever, constantly, continually*.

> *She's always whining about something.*
> *He's forever laughing and making silly comments.*

The past continuous tense

Typical forms of this tense are as shown in:

> *I was winning.*   **but not** *I was liking it.*
> *She was winning.*
> *They were winning.*

> *Was I winning?*
> *Was she winning?*
> *Were you winning?*

> *I was not winning*   **but not** *I was not liking it.*
> *We were not winning.*
> *They weren't winning.*

Some main verbs are not normally used in the continuous in standard British English, though they may be used this way in other varieties of English. These are generally verbs about states rather than feelings.

We use the past continuous tense in these ways:

– with a time expression, such as *at 6p.m. yesterday*, to talk about an action that began before that time and finished after it. The exact length of time the action took is not important.

> *What **were you doing** at eight o'clock last night? –*
>   *I **was standing** at the bus stop.*

– to talk about an interrupted action. Note that for the event that interrupts the action, we use the past simple tense.

> *We **were** all **sitting** in our places when the bell **rang**.*

— to talk about a short action that happened whilst a longer one was already taking place.

> *While I was waiting for the bus I dropped my purse.*

— to describe a scene in the past, especially in a story.

> *It was a dreadful morning. The snow was still falling, the wind was blowing, and the cars were skidding on the icy roads.*

The present perfect tense

Typical forms of this tense are as shown in:

I have finished.
He has found them.
They've finished.
They've found her.
Listen! I've heard some great news; Jim's won!
They've bought a brand new car.
You've got a nerve!

Have they finished? – No, they haven't.
Has Mary arrived yet? – No, she hasn't.

I have not finished.
He has not finished.
Ranee hasn't found her bracelet yet.
They haven't seen her.

The contracted forms are:

has = **'s**	have = **'ve**
has not = **hasn't**	have not = **haven't**

The present perfect tense is used to talk about events that are relevant to the present but that happened in the past. It is used to talk about an action that started in the past, without mentioning a specific time.

Her daughter has had an accident.
We have seen the Eiffel Tower and the Arc de Triomphe.

If the present perfect occurs more than once in a compound sentence, the second and subsequent instances of *have* can be left out.

They have bought their tickets and booked their seats.

- We can use *just* if we want to show that the action has very recently been completed.

    They have just bought their tickets.
    He has just finished his homework.

  If the event did not take place you can use *never*. If you want to find out whether it took place or not, you can use *ever*.

    Have you ever been to Greece?
    I've never done anything like this before.

- If we want to indicate a moment in time or a period of time, we can use expressions such as *recently, lately, this morning, today,* or *this week* with the present perfect tense.

    I haven't been to the cinema recently.
    I've waited a week for your answer.

- In questions and negative sentences, the present perfect can be used with *yet*, meaning 'at the time of speaking'. In positive sentences, use *already*.

    Haven't you finished yet?
    Have you bought the tickets yet?
    I've already seen that film.

The present perfect tense is often used to answer the question *How long...?* together with *for* to talk about a period of time, or *since* to talk about duration from a point in time.

    I have lived in Edinburgh for fifteen years.
    How long have you lived in Edinburgh?
    We've had this car since 2008.
    We haven't spoken to each other since the night of the argument.

The past perfect tense

Typical forms of this tense are as shown in:

> *I had misheard.*
> *She had misheard.*
> *I had finished.*
> *She had found them.*
> *She'd gone.*
> *They'd found her.*

> *Had I misheard?*
> *Had it gone?*
> *Had Mary arrived before Peter told you? – No, she **hadn't**.*

> *I had not misheard.*
> *He had misheard.*
> *I had not finished.*
> *It had not worked.*
> *I hadn't realized how serious the problem was.*
> *They hadn't seen her.*

The contracted forms are:

    had = **'d**   had not = **hadn't**

The past perfect tense goes one step further back into the past than the present perfect.

> *Had you ever seen her before then? – No, I **hadn't**.*

The past perfect tense is used to talk about:

– an action that took place in the past before something else took place.

> *She had just made some coffee when I arrived.*

— an action or state that began before another action in the past and continued up to the time of the second action and perhaps even beyond that time.

> *Ashraf had already known my brother for two years when I met him.*

• It is often used in the main clause of a complex sentence, to set the scene for a past event.

> *We had always wanted to visit Canada for a long time, so last year we decided to go.*

• It is often used with a time expression such as *always* or *for several days*.

> *We had always wanted to visit Canada, so last year we decided to go.*

The present perfect continuous tense

Typical forms of this tense are as shown in:

> *I have been waiting.*
> *I've been waiting.*
> *She has been waiting.*
> *She's been waiting.*

> *Have I been snoring?*
> *Has he been waiting?*
> *Have you been waiting long?*

> *I have not been waiting.*
> *She has not been waiting.*

We use the present perfect continuous tense to talk about:

- actions and states that began in the past and are still continuing at the time of speaking.

> *I have been holding this ladder for ages. When are you going to come down?*

- actions and states that began in the past and have only just finished.

> *Thank goodness you're here! I've been waiting for hours.*

- repeated actions.

> *I've been getting this magazine every week for a year.*

There is sometimes little difference between the meaning of the present perfect and the meaning of the present perfect continuous when they are used for long-term actions.

> *I have been working here for three years.*
> *I have worked here for three years.*

We usually choose the continuous form for more temporary actions or states.

> *I have been living in London since I left school.*

... and the present perfect form for more permanent ones.

> *I have lived in London since I was born.*

- We cannot use this tense with verbs such as *be*, *know*, and *like*, which are not used in continuous forms.

- We can use *for* and *since* with the continuous form in the same way as with the present perfect form. See also pp. 98–101 for more about continuous uses of the verb.

> *I have been studying English for three years.*
> *I have studied English for three years.*

> *I have been living in London since I left school.*
> *I have lived in London since I was born.*

The past perfect continuous tense

Typical forms of this tense are as shown in:

> *I had been waiting.*
> *I'd been waiting.*
> *She had been waiting.*
> *She'd been waiting.*

> *Had I been talking nonsense? What had I said?*
> *Had he been waiting long?*
> *Had you been expecting to meet Mary at the station?*

> *I had not been waiting.*
> *She had not been waiting.*
> *They hadn't been looking very carefully.*

The past perfect continuous tense is used to talk about an action which began before another action in the past and either:

– continued up to the time of the second action,

> *I hadn't been waiting long when a lorry drew up beside me.*

– or was completed before the second action happened.

> *I had been studying and decided to take a stroll to clear my mind.*
> *We had been cleaning the car for hours, so we stopped and had a drink.*

• The past perfect continuous is often used in the main clause of a complex sentence, to set the scene for an event.

> *I had been driving for about an hour when I heard a noise in the engine.*

- The past perfect continuous is often used to talk about a repeated action.

  She had been trying to telephone her mother all day.

  Remember that you cannot use the past perfect continuous with verbs such as *like*, which are not used in the continuous. See p. 98.

Future reference

Verb forms

English has no future tense as such. However, several forms, especially the **modal** verbs *will* and *shall*, can be used to make future reference. These forms are summarized as follows:

1 *Will/shall* + the **base form** makes the most direct form of future reference. See p. 66. The other modal verbs that express possibility make a more indirect reference to future time.

> *It will take several years to finish.*
> *Jean will look after the dogs while we're away.*
> *I shall simply tell her to mind her own business.*
> *We shall see.*

2 *Be going to* + the **base form** is used to express intention and make predictions. See p. 113.

> *He failed his exam last year; this year he is going to work harder.*
> *You'd better take the washing in; it is going to rain.*

3 The **present continuous tense** is used to talk about plans and arrangements in the future with a time adverb. See p. 98.

> *Sarah and Harriet are meeting at ten o'clock on Tuesday.*
> *I am flying to Glasgow on Friday.*

4 The **present simple tense** is used with a time adverb to talk about future plans which are part of a timetable or previous arrangement. See p. 94.

> *The main film starts at 2.45 p.m.*
> *We leave at 4 p.m. tomorrow.*

5 The **future perfect tense** (*will have* + the **past participle**) is used with a time adverb to talk about an action that will be finished at the time in the future that you are referring to. See p. 115.

> *I was hoping to meet James, but by the time I arrive he will have gone home.*

6 *Be about to* + the **base form** is used to talk about the very near future. See p. 116.

> *I'm sorry I can't stop and chat; I'm about to leave for work.*

7 The **future continuous tense** (*will be* + the **present participle**) is used to talk about future action in progress. See p. 117.

> *What will you be doing on Saturday morning? Oh, I'll be shopping as usual.*

8 *Be to* + the **base form** is used to talk about formal plans, especially in journalism. See p. 117.

> *The President is to attend an EU–Russia summit tomorrow.*

1 *will/shall*
The modal verbs *will* or *shall* followed by the **base form** of a main verb are used to express future reference.

I shall come.	*We shall come.*
or	or
I will come.	*We will come.*
You will come.	*You will come.*
She/he/it will come.	*They will come.*

Will can be used with all persons of the verb, although some speakers prefer to use *shall* in the 1st person singular and plural. See p. 66 for further details.

- The contracted form is *'ll* for both verbs, so there is no difference in informal speech.

    I'll probably be late, but I expect they'll be on time.

    The contracted negative forms are *won't* and *shan't*.

    We won't come.
    We shan't come.

- If there are two verbs in the sentence, it is normal not to repeat the modal form before the second one.

    I won't go see him or speak to him for six months.

We use *will* (or *shall*) for future reference in the following ways:

- to talk about future facts.

    I shan't see Mary next week.
    I'll be on the plane this time tomorrow.

- to make promises or reassurances.

    I'll be home in time for tea.
    This won't happen again, I can assure you.

- to announce a decision that the speaker has just made.

    Er, I'll have the pizza Margherita and a side salad, please.
    Right, I shall ask him, and see if his story matches yours.

- to express negative intention, using *won't*.

    I won't go there again. The service was dreadful.

– to express refusal.

> I **won't put up with** any more of this silly behaviour.
> I've tried to persuade her but she **won't come**.

– to talk about an event in the future, possibly in the distant future. A time clause may be used.

> People **will be** amazed when they hear about this in years to come.

– to refer to inevitable actions or events that will take place in the future.

> Christmas is past, but it **will come** again next year.

– to express an opinion about a future event after verbs such as believe, expect, hope, know, and think.

> I **expect** he'll **be** home soon.
> I **hope** you'll **be** very happy in your new home.

– to express a real possibility in conditional sentences. See p. 273.

> If you phone after six I'll **tell** you all about it.

2 **be going to**

Future reference can be made with be + going to + the **base form** of a main verb.

> I **am going to** wait.
> He **is going to** wait.
> I **am not going to** wait.
> He **is not going to** wait.
> Is he **going to** wait?
> Are they **going to** wait?

Be going to is used in the following ways:

– to express intention about the future.

> *Mary isn't going to study art; she's going to be a nurse.*

– to talk about things that have already been decided.

> *Is Jim going to leave his job? – Yes, he is.*
> *Where's Mary? She said she was going to come early.*

– to make a prediction about the future, often the very near future, based on something in the present.

> *Watch the milk! It is going to boil over!*
> *Sally never does any work; she is going to fail her exams.*

If the past tense of *be* is used, a past intention or prediction can be expressed.

> *Judy was going to meet me, but she was ill and couldn't come.*
> *She was obviously going to get blisters with those new shoes.*

Note this difference:

Be going to is usually used for future events where the speaker expresses his or her intention.
Will is used to express decisions made at the moment of speaking.

> *I'm going to go to the pictures on Friday; would you like to come?*
> *Yes, I'll go if Chris goes.*

3 Present continuous

The present continuous tense is used to talk about plans for the future, or specific arrangements that people have made for future events.

> *The school is having a sale next week; I'm running the bookstall.*

It is often used in questions about future arrangements.

> *What are you doing on Saturday? – I'm going to a football match with Peter.*
> *When are you leaving? – At the end of term.*

If there are two verbs in the sentence, it is normal not to repeat the auxiliary before the second and subsequent ones.

> *We are meeting at 12.30 p.m., having a quick lunch, and starting work at 1.15.*

4 Present simple

The present simple tense is also used to talk about events that form part of a timetable or programme.

> *The train leaves Edinburgh at 10.10 a.m. and arrives in London at 3.20 p.m.*
> *These are the arrangements for Friday: doors open at 7 p.m., the Mayor arrives at 7.30 p.m., and the meeting starts at 7.45 p.m.*

5 The future perfect (*will have* + **the past participle of a main verb**)

This form is used to talk about an action that will be complete at a time in the future that you are talking about. It is often used with verbs relating to finishing or completing.

The contracted positive form is *'ll have* or *will've*.

> *Can you come round next Saturday? – Yes, I'll have finished
>   my exams by then.*
> *Dad will've made dinner by the time we get back.*

The contracted negative is **won't have**.

> *The essay is due on Tuesday, but I won't have completed it by
>   then.*

In questions, the subject comes after *will*. The short answer to a
question is *will* without the past participle.

> *Will you have finished dinner by then? – Yes, we will.*

6 *be + about to +* **the base form**

The appropriate form of *be + about to +* the **base form** of a main verb
is used to talk about events in the very near future.

> *Turn off the gas – the soup is about to boil over.*
> *Come on! The film's about to start!*

It is sometimes used with *just* following the *be* word to give even
more immediacy.

> *Quick, jump in! The train is (just) about to leave.*

Be about to can also be used in the **past** to suggest that someone is
on the point of carrying out an action when it is interrupted. In this
case it is usually followed by *when*.

> *They were (just) about to go to bed when the phone rang.*

7 **The future continuous tense**
This is made with *will* + *be* + the **present participle** of a main verb.
Will be forms negatives, contractions, questions, and short answers
in the usual way.

The future continuous is used in a rather informal way to suggest
that something is about to happen or will happen at some time that
is not clear or precise.

> *I'll be seeing you.*
> *We'll be getting in touch with you.*
> *They'll be wanting us to clean our own classrooms next!*
> *We won't be seeing Uncle John while we are in Australia.*

It is also used to talk about an activity that will already be in
progress at a particular time in the future.

> *Will you be working here next week?*
> *No, I won't. I'll be starting my new job.*
> *Just think! This time next week, we will be flying to Sydney.*

8 *be to* + **the base form**
The appropriate form of *be* + *to* + the **base form** of a main verb is
used mainly in fairly formal English to talk about plans, arrangements,
and instructions. It indicates that what will happen is part of an
expected process, and is often found in journalistic texts.

> *Foreign ministers of the NATO countries are to meet in Brussels*
> *next week.*
> *The President has left for Geneva, where he is to attend the*
> *meeting.*

Active and passive

Active sentences

In the following example, the verb is **active**.

> *The postman delivers hundreds of letters every day.*

The subject of an active sentence is also the person or thing that carries out the action. We use the active when the subject of the verb is the doer of the action. The active is used in most English speech and writing, because we usually want to inform our listener or our reader who or what carried out the action of the verb.

> *He hid the money under the bed.*
> *The car knocked over a pedestrian.*
> *I'm sending the book by express delivery.*

Passive sentences

In the following example, the verb is in the **passive**.

> *Thousands of letters are delivered every day.*

The subject in a passive sentence is not the person or thing that does the action of the verb. It is the person or thing that is acted on by the verb.

> *The injured man was helped by a passer-by.*
> *The man was being questioned by the police.*
> *The patient was operated on by a team of five surgeons.*

The passive is made with the appropriate form of *be* + the **past participle** of the main verb.

- We use the passive to direct our listener's attention to the important part of our message. For instance, in the first example of this section we do not need to know who delivers the letters, so all mention of the postman is left out.

- The passive can be used when we do not know who carries out the action expressed by the verb, or when it is not important that we should know. It is sometimes much more important to know what has happened than who or what did it.

> *The money was hidden under the bed.*
> *The book is being sent by express delivery.*
> *An elderly man was run over while crossing the road.*
> *Roger has been given his promotion.*
> *The patient was operated on.*

The passive allows us to select the parts of a sentence to which we want to draw attention. It can be used when we want to focus on:

– the **agent**, i.e. who brought the action about. We show the agent with *by*.

> *The window was broken by some boys.*
> *My brother was given extra tuition by his teacher.*
> *The old man was run over by a careless driver.*
> *The patient was operated on by a team of top surgeons.*

– the **instrument**, i.e. what was used to make the action happen. We show the instrument with *by* or *with*.

> *The sorting is done by machine.*
> *The safe was blown open with dynamite.*
> *The old man was knocked over by a bus.*
> *I was showered with presents on my eighteenth birthday.*

  – the **means**, i.e. what caused the action to happen. We show the means with *by* or *with*.

> *The window was shattered by the explosion.*
> *He was exhausted with the strain of caring for his elderly parents.*
> *Spelling errors are marked with a cross in the margin.*
> *He was taken to hospital by ambulance.*

The subject of a passive verb

The verb in a passive sentence has the word that would normally be its object in the position of the subject. When a verb has two objects, either the indirect object or the direct object of the active verb may become the subject of the passive verb.

> *I've been offered a place at university.*
> *We were given a second chance.*

If the indirect object is mentioned after the passive verb, the sentence must use *to*.

> *The building has been sold to property developers.*
> *The medal is awarded to students who have shown academic excellence.*

Some verbs that are often used this way are: *give, offer, lend, promise, sell,* and *tell*.

Form of the passive

Passive verbs are made from a form of *be* + the **past participle** of a main verb. In the passive, the form of the auxiliary verb *be* indicates the tense.

> *They sell cheap computer games here.*
> *Cheap computer games are sold here.*
> *They took him to the police station for questioning.*
> *He was taken to the police station for questioning.*

- Some verbs are only or mostly used in the passive, e.g. *be born* and *be deemed*.

> *The film was deemed unsuitable for younger audiences.*
> *My brother and I were born in Wales.*

The impersonal passive

This form of the passive sentence is useful when you want to report what is or was generally understood or accepted by a group of people.

> *The suitcase was found to be empty.*
> *The money is thought to be missing.*
> *The rumour is believed to be true.*

The form *it* + **passive** + **that** can be used when you do not want to mention the source of a report or rumour.

> *It is reported that over a hundred people died in the explosion.*
> *It is said that his income is over £200 a minute.*

The passive with *get*

In informal English, a type of passive is sometimes made with *get* instead of *be*.

> *How did that teapot get broken?*
> *Our cat got run over last week.*

Get is also used to form a small set of passive verbs in contexts which are not informal (or 'neutral'), e.g. *get dressed*, *get married*, *get lost*.

> *Harriet got lost on the Underground.*
> *When are you two getting married?*

The causative passive with *have*

There is another kind of verbal group that is like the passive, because the person who carries out the action of the main verb is not the person who is the subject of the clause. It expresses the idea that the subject caused or ordered someone to take the action mentioned.

> *We are having the garage door replaced.*
> *She had her hair cut short.*
> *They did not have the carpet cleaned after all.*

It has the form: *have* + **direct object** + **past participle**.

Compare:

Ralph repaired his car = Ralph did the work.
Ralph had his car repaired = He paid someone else to do the work.

Finite and non-finite verbs

In a sentence, there is normally at least one verb that has both a **subject** and a **tense**. When a verb has a subject and a tense, it can be referred to as a **finite** verb.

> *We want Charlie to act as club secretary.*
> *I like taking photographs of insects.*
> *Coming home last night, I saw a deer run across the road.*

Some forms of a verb are referred to as **non-finite**. The **present** and **past participles** and the *to* **infinitive** are the most common of these. The base form is often used in a non-finite way. Every verb can be used in a clause in either a **finite** or **non-finite** way.

- A verb is finite if it is found in a clause in combination with a subject and a tense.

> *I walked home.*
> *We saw a deer.*
> *They appreciate a little praise now and then.*

- It is non-finite if it is used:

- without the verb having a tense.

> *To open, tear off the tab.*
> *Looking around, he noticed a letter on the floor.*
> *Worn out by the heat, they stopped for a drink.*

- with no agreement between the subject (if there is one) and the verb.

> *That plan failing, he gave up.*
> *Our guests departed, we felt a little depressed.*

A compound verb is actually made up of one finite part, which is always the first auxiliary verb, while the remaining non-finite parts are the base form or the participles.

In the following examples the finite part of the verb phrase is in blue italic:

> I *may* have been joking *when I said that.*
> Helen *was* running *around screaming.*
> I *had* been living *in a dream for months.*
> Olivia *is* coming *round at 6 o'clock this evening.*

The present simple and past simple forms of a verb are always finite.

> I *sing.*
> We *tell stories at night.*
> Maya *laughed.*
> The shelter *collapsed.*

- A non-finite verb is sometimes used immediately after a finite verb.

> I *like* to get up *early at the weekend.*
> Harriet really *dislikes* cleaning *the cooker.*
> I certainly *wouldn't want* to see *him again.*
> We *persuaded them* to join *us.*

Often a noun or pronoun can come between the finite verb and the non-finite one. See p. 128 and p. 129 for more on this.

> We *want Charlie* to act *as club secretary.*
> She *wanted him* to wash *his hands in the bathroom.*
> I *don't like you* cleaning *your boots over the sink.*

- When the second verb is an *-ing* form coming after a noun or pronoun, there can be a difference in grammar between two similar sentences. Both sentences below are acceptable, although the first example might seem ambiguous to some people. In the second sentence, the *-ing* form is used as a verbal noun. See also p. 130.

  She didn't like him cleaning his boots over the sink.
  She didn't like his cleaning his boots over the sink.

The non-finite parts of the verb

Non-finite parts of a verb are those that do not indicate number, person or tense. The common non-finite forms are:

- the **base form**
- the **present participle** or -*ing* form
- the **past participle**
- the *to* **infinitive**

There are also other non-finite forms, such as:

- the **continuous** *to* **infinitive**: *to be teaching*
- the **perfect** *to* **infinitive**: *to have taught*
- the **passive** *to* **infinitive**: *to be taught*

The base form

As well as serving as the verb form on which most of the other parts of the verb are based, the **base form** is frequently used as a non-finite part of the verb. Because of this it is sometimes called the '*bare infinitive*' or the '*infinitive without to*'.

The **base form** is used as a **non-finite** part of the verb in these ways:

- after modal verbs.

    You must stop at the kerb before you cross.
    He should think before he speaks.

- after *let's* (suggestion) and *let* (permission) and *make* (compulsion).

    Let's invite Annette round for dinner.
    Let the cat go!
    Make him stop!
    Let him finish what he was saying!

– after *feel, hear, see, watch* + an object.

> *I heard* him *run downstairs.*
> *Later we saw* them *leave the house.*

– after a *to* infinitive to which it is joined by *and*.

> *I want you to sit and listen.*
> *Just wait and see.*

– after *would rather* and *had better*.

> *I would rather go out, but I think we had better stay home and*
> *finish the painting.*

Verbs of perception may be followed either by the **base form** or by the
-ing form. There is often a change of sentence meaning.

These verbs include: *see, hear, feel, smell, listen to, watch.*

> *We watched her park the car = we watched the whole event.*
> *We watched her parking the car = we may only have seen part*
> *of the event.*
> *I heard a cuckoo call = I heard just one call.*
> *We heard the birds singing = We heard part of the song of*
> *the birds.*

The *to* infinitive

The *to* infinitive is used as follows:

- after an adjective of quality such as *small, tall, agreeable, pleasant, funny* that is used in combination with *too*.

  > *The child was too small to reach the switch.*
  > *The knife was too blunt to cut the string.*

  or (*not*) + adjective of quality + *enough*.

  > *The child was not tall enough to reach the switch.*
  > *The knife was not sharp enough to cut the string.*
  > *I was stupid enough to go walking in flip flops.*

- after adjectives of emotion such as: *angry, happy, glad, sad, sorry, surprised*, to express the reason for the emotion.

  > *I'm glad to see you.*
  > *I'm sorry to hear your news.*

- after a 'behaviour' adjective such as: *good, kind, nice, silly, wrong,* (sometimes + *of* + another **noun phrase**).

  > *It was good of you to come, and kind of Jane to have sent those flowers.*
  > *It was silly to go off like that.*
  > *It was kind of you to ring me.*

- after a **WH-** word such as: *how, what, where, whether, which, who, whom*.

  > *We have no idea what to get for Tim's birthday.*
  > *I don't know where to go.*
  > *I can't think how to do it.*
  > *They were wondering who to see first.*

– after a noun phrase such as *a good idea, a good thing, a mistake* (sometimes + *for* + another **noun phrase**).

> *It was a mistake* for Jim *to buy* that motorbike.
> *It was a good idea to stop* here.

– after an adjective such as *easy, difficult, hard, impossible* + *for* + **noun phrase**.

> *It has never been easy* for David *to sit* exams.

– after a verb followed by *for*, e.g. *ask, wait* + *for* + **noun phrase**.

> *They are waiting* for us *to decide*.

• The *to* infinitive can be used to express purpose or necessity after a verb followed by a pronoun or a noun.

purpose: I brought *it* **to read** on the train = so that I could read it.
necessity: There is *work* **to do**! = work that must be done.

Sometimes the particle *to* can be used alone, provided the meaning is clear, for example in a short response, when the whole verb form is used in a previous sentence or clause.

> *Did you **meet** Tina? No, I wanted* **to***, but she was ill.*
> *Are you going to **visit** the museum? Yes, we hope* **to***.*

The *to* infinitive and the *-ing* form

The *to* infinitive and the *-ing* form (the present participle) can each be used after certain verbs.

Verbs followed by the *to* infinitive include: *agree, arrange, attempt, choose, decide, fail, hope, learn, manage, offer, plan, seem.*

> *I agreed to help Shona with her homework.*
> *The driver attempted to remove the flat tyre.*
> *I hope to see you again at the next meeting.*

Verbs followed by an **object** + the *to* **infinitive** include: *advise, allow, command, forbid, force, invite, order, persuade, remind, teach, tell.*

> *Peter advised Ron to call the police.*
> *Esther reminded her teacher to set some revision.*

Verbs that can be followed *either* directly by the *to* **infinitive** *or* by an **object** + the *to* **infinitive** include: *ask, expect, help, intend, like, love, hate, mean, prefer, want, wish.*

> *I certainly intended to go to the party.*
> *We really expected Sally to pass the exam.*

> Note this difference:
> *I want to have a cat = It will be my cat.*
> *I want her to have a cat = It will be her cat.*
> *Dad likes to wash the car = Dad washes the car.*
> *Dad likes John to wash the car = John washes the car.*

Verbs followed by the *-ing* form include: *avoid, be used to, delay, dislike, escape, finish, forgive, give up, go on, imagine.*

> *I usually avoid going into town late at night.*
> *Miriam hates peeling potatoes.*
> *Have you finished reading that book yet?*

- Some verbs may be followed either by the *to* infinitive or by the
  -ing form with little or no change in meaning. These verbs include:
  begin, start, cease, continue, intend, like, love, hate, prefer.

  > *He began to run around shouting.*
  > *He began running around shouting.*
  > *She likes to swim in the sea.*
  > *She likes swimming in the sea.*
  > *I can't bear to see violence.*
  > *I can't bear seeing violence.*

- Some verbs may be followed either by the *to* infinitive or by the
  -ing form but the meaning of the sentence changes depending
  on the form that is used. These verbs include: *try, forget, remember.*

  > *I remembered to switch the lights off before we went out.*
  > *I remember switching the lights off before we went out.*
  > *She tried to talk to him, but his secretary wouldn't put the call
  >   through.*
  > *She tried talking to him, but he wouldn't listen.*

Particularly after verbs such as *go* and *come*, the *to* infinitive is
understood to express purpose.

> *She has gone to do the shopping.*
> *They came here to learn English.*

Use of the verb followed by the *-ing* form concentrates on what happens.
The second verb is really the object of the first one. These verbs include:
remember, forget, try.

> *I definitely remember switching the lights off before we
>   went out.*
> *She tried talking to him, but he wouldn't listen.*

Some **set expressions** (idioms) are followed by *-ing*. These include: *it's not worth*, and *it's no fun*.

> *It's no fun going out alone.*
> *It's no use phoning him; he's gone away.*
> *It's worth trying one more time.*

The noun phrase

A noun phrase is a word or group of words that can function as the **subject**, the **object**, or the **complement** in a sentence.

> *The manager interviewed all the applicants on Tuesday.*
> *Lydia was the successful applicant.*

See pp. 18–19 and pp. 230–231 for more information about these functions. A noun phrase must always contain a noun or a pronoun.

A noun phrase may consist of only one word. That word will be either a noun or a pronoun.

> *Mary left late.*
> *She left late.*
> *Cheese is expensive.*
> *It is expensive.*

A noun phrase may consist of more than one word. One of these words, a noun or a pronoun, is the **headword**. The other words describe or modify the headword.

> *the tall girl*
> *the very tall girl*
> *a strikingly beautiful girl*
> *the tall girl with green eyes*

Words that go before the headword are called **premodifiers**. A noun can be premodified by:

– a determiner. See p. 160.

> *the girl*　　　　*that boy*
> *a spider*　　　　*some rice*

– one or more adjectives. See pp. 160–190.

> *tall girls*
> *tall dark girls*
> *tall dark handsome men*

– a number, another noun, or the present participle or past participle of a verb.

> *three days*
> *the railway station buffet*
> *an annoying habit*
> *an overworked man*

Words that go after the headword are called **postmodifiers**. A noun can be postmodified by:

– a prepositional phrase (a noun phrase with a preposition in front of it).

> *the person in the corner*
> *the view across the valley*
> *the house opposite the church*
> *creatures under the sea*

– a subordinate clause (usually one beginning with *who*, *which* or *that*). See p. 264.

> *All the women who had gathered there finally went away.*
> *Milk that has been kept too long can go sour.*

– less commonly, certain adjectives. See p. 160.

> *the princess royal*
> *the president elect*

- Personal pronouns are only rarely premodified or postmodified. See p. 203.

> *Silly me.*
> *Poor old you.*

Types of noun

Nouns can be classified according to what they refer to.

- Nouns that are really names are called **proper nouns**. Proper nouns usually refer to a particular named person or thing.

They include:

- the names of specific people.

    Anna Dickinson   *John Lennon*
    Lucy White   *Mrs Merton*

- geographical items.

    Spain   *Mount Everest*
    China   *England*
    The Thames   *Paris*
    Covent Garden   *Balcombe Road*

- days of the week, months, and annual Church festivals.

    Thursday   *June*
    Christmas   *Easter*

- patented goods and trade names.

    Hoover   *Persil*
    Jaguar   *Samsung*

- newspaper and magazine titles.

    The Times   *Vogue*
    The New Scientist   *Time Out*

– shop, cinema, theatre names, buildings.

> *The Odeon*   *Next*
> *The Royal Mews*   *Abbey National*

– titles (the polite or professional labels that we give to people).

> *Doctor* Johnson   *Sir* George Hardie.
> *Professor* James   **President** Sarkozy

A person's title is usually placed before his or her name.
Proper nouns and titles are always written with an initial
capital letter.

- All the other nouns that refer to things or species are called
  common nouns.

> *I put the **tennis balls** in that **basket** there.*
> *My **brother** and **sister** visited my **mother**.*
> *The **anger** that John felt was overwhelming.*

Common nouns can be divided into the following groups, according
to their meaning:

Abstract nouns. These refer to intangible items.

> *honesty*   *anger*
> *idea*   *time*
> *ugliness*   *behaviour*

Concrete nouns. These refer to tangible items.

> *pig*   *granite*
> *table*   *butcher*
> *brother*   *sugar*

A concrete noun may refer to a living thing (**animate** nouns) or a physical object (**inanimate** nouns).

Collective nouns. These refer to collections of people or animals.

> *a herd of cows*
> *a swarm of bees*

Nouns may also be classified according to the words with which they are used, that is:

- whether or not the noun gives us information about **singular** and **plural number**.

- the other words that can be used in the same noun phrase.

This gives us a useful distinction between **countable nouns** and **uncountable nouns**.

Countable nouns refer to things that we can count: *one cat, two cats, seventeen cats,* and so on. They have singular and plural forms, which are shown by the spelling. They must be used with a determiner if they are singular.

> *Dogs ran wild in the streets.*
> *The dog is loose again.*
> *Fetch a chair for Maddy, will you?*
> *We've bought six new chairs.*

Uncountable nouns refer to:

- things that are not normally thought of as countable.

> *John asked me for some advice.*
> *Anna gave us some more information about her work.*
> *Homework occupied much of Sonia's evening.*

– qualities or abstract ideas.

> *Our knowledge of outer space is increasing daily.*
> *Trevor gave evidence at the trial.*
> *Anger is a normal human emotion.*

Uncountable nouns do not usually have a plural form. They are followed by a singular verb. They are not normally used with the indefinite article. (You cannot talk about *'an advice'* or *'a money'*.) When it is necessary to think of an item as countable it has to be used with a **partitive noun**. See p. 141.

> *He bought seven sheets of cardboard.*
> *Let me give you a piece of advice.*

Some examples of the commonest uncountable nouns are: *advice, anger, beauty, behaviour, conduct, despair, evidence, furniture, happiness, homework, information, safety, knowledge, leisure, money, news, progress, research, jumble.*

• Verbal nouns (p. 158), which are formed from the present participle of verbs, can also be used as uncountable nouns.

> *Why don't you try walking to work?*
> *Brian was told to stop smoking.*
> *The ringing in his ears continued.*

> Note that nouns that are uncountable in English may be countable in other languages. See p. 142.

Mass nouns

These are nouns that refer to a substance that can be divided or measured but not counted, e.g. *sugar, water*. They do not usually have an indefinite article in front.

> *Meat is usually more expensive than cheese.*
> *Sugar is quite cheap.*

Mass nouns only take a plural in special cases. They can be counted when they refer to:

– a particular type or types of the substance.

> *There was a buffet of bread and rolls, cheese, cold meats and tea or coffee.*
> *Ros brought out a tempting selection of French cheeses.*
> *The principal sugars are glucose, sucrose, and fructose.*

– a serving of the substance.

> *Two teas, please.*
> *He went up to the bar and ordered two lagers.*

• Mass nouns are often used together with a partitive noun.

> *There are only two pieces of furniture in the room.*
> *There are three portions of meat in this special pack.*
> *Five pints of lager, please.*

Partitive nouns

Partitive nouns are commonly followed by *of*. They are used when we need to talk about a part of a mass noun or when we need to count the quantity of something that is referred to by an uncountable noun or a mass noun, especially when it is necessary to talk about:

– measurements and quantities with mass nouns.

> *three pieces of toast*   *a slice of cheese*
> *a bit of fluff*   *two spoonfuls of sugar*

– individual items with uncountable nouns.

> *Two pieces of furniture needed major repairs.*
> *We needed several lengths of string.*

– a collection of countable nouns.

> *The road was blocked by a flock of sheep.*
> *He has a small herd of dairy cows.*
> *There was a crowd of football supporters of the bus.*
> *A couple of cats were fighting.*

> Many collective nouns can be used as partitive nouns.
> See p. 138.

Nouns that have both countable and uncountable uses

Most nouns are either countable nouns or uncountable nouns, as
explained on p. 138. Some nouns, however, behave like countable
nouns in some sentences and uncountable nouns in other sentences.
They usually have different meanings depending on how they are used.
For example *time*, *light*, *history*, *space*, *laugh*, and *grocery* have more than
one meaning.

> *Time passed slowly.*
> *She did it four times.*
> *Light travels faster than sound.*
> *The lights in this room are too bright.*
> *The rocket was launched into space.*
> *There are plenty of empty spaces on the shelves.*

Some nouns that are countable nouns in other languages are used
only as uncountable nouns in English, e.g. *information*, *advice*.

> *He received all the necessary information.*
> *I don't need your help.*

Some nouns are used only in the plural form, even when we are talking
about one item, e.g. *trousers*, *clothes*, *jeans*. We can use a partitive noun
with *of* when referring to a single item.

> *These trousers need cleaning.*
> *Put the scissors back when you have finished with them.*
> *I need* a pair of *pliers.*
> *Liz gathered up* a bundle of *clothes.*

Gender of nouns

In some languages, nouns have **gender**. This means that a noun causes other words such as adjectives to change their spelling according to certain rules. Grammatical gender has little to do with biological gender. English does not have **grammatical gender** for nouns.

On the other hand, the **biological gender** of the thing or person referred to does affect a few areas of English grammar.

> *a cow... she or it*   *a bull... he or it*
> *a girl... she*   *a boy... he*

Gender distinctions are relevant where personal pronouns (p. 203) and possessive determiners (p. 160) have to be decided on. These distinctions are only noticeable in **singular** nouns.

> *He found his book.*
> *He had been looking for it.*
> *She found her book.*
> *She had been looking for it.*

There are also special cases, such as the association of neuter gender with babies and small animals, or feminine gender with a vehicle.

> *I just saw a mouse. It was running across the room.*
> *The spider was spinning its web.*
> *The beetle crawled into its hole.*
> *The baby threw down its rattle.*
> *I've got a new boat; she's a real beauty.*

Nouns denoting male persons and animals are **masculine** in that they are used with the pronouns and possessive determiners *he, him, his*.

Nouns denoting female persons and animals are **feminine** in that they are used with the pronouns and possessive determiners *she, her, hers*.

Barry saw Linda. He called out to her that he had found her book.
Marcia saw Paul. She called out to him that she had found his book.
Madeleine saw Kim. She said 'Hello' to her.

The pronouns and possessive determiners used to refer to common or **neuter** nouns are: *it, its.*

The truth will emerge. It always does.

Nouns denoting inanimate objects and abstract notions are also neuter.

• Some nouns denoting people have the same form for masculine and feminine. Nouns used for a group, e.g. *government* or *team*, have **common** or **neuter** gender, even when we know that the group is made up exclusively of male or female members.

The government has changed its policy.
The team has won its first medal at a major championship.

With some nouns of common gender it might be possible to specify the gender if we had sufficient information. But if we do not have this knowledge, the choice of pronoun or possessive determiner becomes a problem.

a driver...he/she
the cook...he/she
doctor...he/she

As a way around this problem, in informal and spoken English, *their* is sometimes used after a singular noun or an indefinite pronoun. See p. 202. Many people consider this grammatically unacceptable, but it is widely used to avoid repetitions of *his or her* or *him or her.*

Each student must apply to his or her tutor for an extension.
Everyone must apply to their tutor for an extension.
Someone has left their coat in my room.

The specialized terms used to name male, female and neutered animals show a number of gender differences.

horse	mare	stallion	gelding
–	cow	bull	steer
sheep	ewe	ram	–

Gender differences are also shown in the nouns that indicate relationships.

parent	mother	father
child	daughter	son

- Many nouns denoting an occupation have no explicit gender.

engineer	doctor	programmer
mechanic	lawyer	driver

Some occupations and professions have a special feminine form for the noun.

Call your bank manager today.
Sue is manageress of a hairdressing salon.
Authors from all over the UK attended the ceremony.
Here in the studio to talk about her new book is authoress Mary Farrell.

Many people prefer to avoid these forms, regarding the distinction as unnecessary.

J.K. Rowling is a highly successful author.
Judi Dench is one of our finest actors.
Michelle Stewart has been promoted to Branch Manager.

Some speakers prefer to use a different form of the word or an entirely different word in order to avoid a gender-marked noun.

the chairman   *the chairperson*   *the chair*

If necessary, the gender of a common noun can be made clear by adding a descriptive term such as *woman* or *male/female*.

Would you prefer to see a woman doctor?
Male staff should use locker room B.

If we are discussing a country from an emotional, economic, or political viewpoint we sometimes use feminine gender.

Poland has made steady progress restructuring her economy.

Showing possession through nouns

Possession can be shown in two ways:

> *The man was mending his car.*
> *The car was being mended by a man.*

– by adding -'s to a singular noun, or an irregular plural noun that does not end in -s.

> | *one dog* | *one boy* | *several children* |
> |---|---|---|
> | *the dog's bones* | *the boy's books* | *the children's toys* |

– by adding -' to a plural noun.

> | *more than one dog* | *more than one boy* |
> |---|---|
> | *the dogs' bones* | *the boys' books* |

There is also the *of* **possessive** (a phrase with *of* followed by a noun).

> | *the side of the ship* | *the end of the queue* |
> |---|---|

The *of* **possessive** is not just a different way of saying the same thing as the -'s possessive.

> *the boy's pencil* but not *the pencil of the boy*

The -'s possessive is generally used only with nouns referring to animate items (e.g. people and animals) and in time phrases.

> | *the driver's foot* | *the dog's nose* |
> |---|---|
> | *today's newspaper* | *a week's holiday* |

The *of* possessive is generally used with nouns referring to inanimate things (i.e. objects) and abstract ideas.

> *the leg of the table*   *the arm of the sofa*
> *the wheel of the car*   *the foot of the bed*
> *the world of ideas*   *the power of thought*

The function of the possessive form in English is to:

– show possession.

> *the boy's books*   *the dog's blanket*

– show a relationship, with a person either as the originator, or the user of the thing named.

> *her parents' consent*   *the student's letter*
> *a women's club*   *the children's park*

– indicate that a place is where someone works or lives.

> *a grocer's*   *the butcher's*
> *a solicitor's*   *my aunt's*

– show that something is a part of a whole.

> *the leg of the table*   *the dog's nose*
> *the wheel of the car*   *the girl's shoulder*

– add a descriptive element which premodifies a noun. It is a type of determiner. See also p. 160.

> *writer's cramp*   *A Winter's Tale*

Rules for the formation of the possessive -'s (apostrophe -s) and -s' (-s apostrophe) are as follows:

– most singular nouns add an apostrophe + -s.

> *a girl's ring*   *a cat's face*

– most plural nouns add an apostrophe after the plural form -s.

> *the boys' football*   *five young girls' faces*

There are exceptions for the following:

– common nouns that end in -s in the singular. When these are made plural the choice of -'s or a simple apostrophe is optional.

> *a cactus*   *the cactus' spines*
> *the cactus's habitat*

– plural nouns not ending in -s, for example those that that have a plural ending in -en. In this case, add an apostrophe + s.

> *children's*   *men's*

– proper nouns and common nouns that end in -s. These usually add -'s in the singular unless the final sound of the basic word is [-iz], in which case, a simple apostrophe is sufficient.

> *Mrs Evans's car*   *Mr Jones's fence*
> *Keats's poetry*   *the Bates's cat*
> *I like Dickens's novels*
> *Peter Bridges' car*

Compound nouns (see p. 151) put the -'s or the simple apostrophe at the end of the complete compound.

> my mother-in-law   my mother-in-law's car
> the runner-up   the runner-up's trophy
> the fire-fighters   the fire-fighters' efforts

Noun phrases that are descriptive of someone's role or profession put the -'s on the headword of the phrase.

> a stock market analyst's annual income
> the senior hospital consultant's weekly visit

If they use an of construction the -'s or simple apostrophe usually goes on the last noun.

> the President of Austria's official car
> the director of marketing's personal assistant

Compound nouns

A compound noun is a noun that is formed from two or more words. The meaning of the whole compound is often different from the meaning of the two words on their own. Compound nouns are very common. The main noun is normally the last one.

teapot	headache
washing machine	driving licence
self-control	CD burner

Compound nouns are commonly formed from the following word combinations:

- noun + noun,
- verb + noun,
- adjective + noun,
- phrasal verb used as noun,
- particle + noun.

noun + noun:	boyfriend	skinhead
verb + noun:	breakfast	grindstone
adjective + noun:	software	hardware
phrasal verb:	a break-in	a take-over
particle + noun:	onlooker	aftershave

The term **particle** is used for a word which could be either an adverb or a preposition.

Compound nouns can be written:

– as one word.

> bookcase   wallpaper
> birdcage   snowflake

– as two words.

> post office   fire engine
> eye shadow   cough sweets

– with a hyphen.

> window-cleaner   air-conditioning
> lamp-post   tee-shirt

Consult a dictionary to discover how the word is normally written. There are often alternative forms to be found, for example, *drop down menu*, *drop-down menu*, and *dropdown menu* are all currently acceptable forms of the same compound noun.

Nouns as modifiers

The compound noun *girlfriend* names a special sort of *friend*. Nouns can also be used as **modifiers** without forming a compound noun.

> a concrete slab   old oak beams
> a car mechanic   a store manager

 A noun that is used as a modifier has the same function as an adjective. The first noun usually makes the second one more specific, but we do not think of it as part of a combination that forms a new word. See p. 186 for more on modifiers.

Number in nouns

Singular number is used when the noun refers to one item.
Plural number is used when the noun refers to more than one item.

Countable nouns have both singular and plural forms.

Uncountable nouns and **mass nouns** do not normally have a plural form. See p. 136 for more on the types of noun.

The regular plural ending of an English noun is -s.

cat   cats

These are the exceptions to the normal pattern:

singular noun ending	plural noun ending
-s, -ss, -ch, -x, -zz focus princess church box buzz	-es focuses princesses churches boxes buzzes
-o hero piano potato	-s or -es heroes pianos potatoes
consonant + y baby hobby	-ies babies hobbies
vowel + y key ray	-s keys rays

singular noun ending	plural noun ending
-f	-s or -ves
hoof	hoofs or hooves
dwarf	dwarfs or dwarves
thief	thieves
roof	roofs
-fe	-ves
knife	knives
life	lives

Irregular plurals

Some nouns have two plural forms.

fish   fish or fishes

Some of them have the same form in the singular and plural.

a sheep   ten sheep
a deer   seven deer

A few change a vowel to form the plural.

man   men
woman   women
foot   feet
mouse   mice

Some nouns form the plural with -en.

child   children
ox   oxen

Since it is not possible to give more than a selection of the irregular forms, you should check in a dictionary if you are in doubt. If the dictionary does not show the plural form, then you can assume that it is regular.

Compound nouns normally form the plural by adding -s to the last word of the compound.

a games console	*three games consoles*
a bookcase	*two bookcases*
an Indian take-away	*two Indian take-aways*

There are a few exceptions:

A compound noun formed from a noun and an adverb makes the first word plural.

a passer-by	*several passers-by*

Compound nouns with *woman* as the first word make both words plural.

a woman doctor	*several women doctors*
a woman driver	*most women drivers*

A compound word which ends in -*ful* normally adds -*s* after -*ful*, but there is an alternative form with the -*s* following the base noun.

a cupful	*three cupfuls/cupsful*
a spoonful	*two spoonfuls/spoonsful*

Plural nouns with singular reference

Some nouns referring to clothes and tools where two equal parts are joined together, e.g. *trousers*, *binoculars*, and *tongs*, are treated as being plural and are followed by a verb in the plural.

My shorts are dirty.
The scissors are on the table.

To talk about one of these items we can use the expression *a pair of...*

John bought a pair of jeans.

To talk about more than one we talk about however many *pairs of...*

Martina bought five pairs of tights.

- When they are used as ordinary numbers, words such as *dozen* and *million* have no plural form.

    nine million stars   *two dozen glasses*

    When they are used to mean a large number, they do have a plural form, which can be used as a partitive.

    There are millions of pebbles on the beach.
    I saw dozens of children in the playground.

Foreign plurals

Nouns that have come into English from foreign languages can:

- keep the plural form of the language they come from.

    an axis   *two axes*
    a crisis   *two crises*

- have plurals formed according to the rules for plural in English.

    a thesaurus   *several thesauruses*
                                 (instead of thesauri)

- have two plurals: one from the foreign language and the other formed according to the rules for plural formation in English. The foreign plural is usually kept for scientific or specialized use.

an index	*some indexes/indices*
a formula	*some formulas/formulae*

Verbal nouns

The **verbal noun** is the -*ing* form, i.e. the present participle of the verb, used as a noun. It can be used in all the places that a noun can be used, but still keeps some characteristics of the verb. It is sometimes called the **gerund**.

> *The screaming of the brakes terrified me.*
> *Smoking is prohibited.*

The verbal noun normally functions as an uncountable noun, as above. However, there are some uses of the verbal noun that can be preceded by an indefinite article or used in the plural.

> *He gave a reading from his latest volume of poetry.*
> *The takings were down this week in the shop.*

The verbal noun can be preceded by the definite article, by adjectives, and by possessives.

> *Her marvellous singing won Helen the scholarship.*

Just like any noun, the verbal noun can function:

– as a **subject**.

> *Driving was impossible.*

– as the **complement** of the verb *be*.

> *Seeing is believing.*
> *His greatest pleasure is working.*

– as an **object** after certain verbs. See also p. 130.

> *Louisa likes swimming but Helen prefers diving.*

– after **prepositions** to make a prepositional phrase.

> *Can you watch them without laughing?*

Verbal nouns are also used:

– after some phrasal verbs such as: *be for/against, give up, keep on, look forward to, put off.*

> *She was all for leaving immediately.*
> *Linda gave up swimming but she kept on dieting.*
> *They were looking forward to writing home.*

– after certain set expressions such as: *can't stand, can't help, it's no use/good.*

> *I can't stand waiting around.*
> *I can't help getting cross.*
> *It's no use crying over spilt milk.*

The **possessive determiner** can be used with the verbal noun, especially in formal English.

> *Anna left the house without my knowing.*

• The verbal noun also has:

– a perfect form: *having ...ed.*

> *Martin was accused of having cheated.*

– a passive form: *being ...ed.*

> *Being asked did not bother me.*

– a perfect passive form: *having been ...ed.*

> *The car showed no sign of having been touched.*

Determiners

Determiners are words that make the reference of nouns more specific. If I say *'this car'* it is clear that I mean a particular car which is near me. If I change it to *'my car'* I am saying something quite specific about ownership.

Determiners can be divided into several kinds according to:

– their meaning.

– what they may go with and where they may come in the noun phrase.

There are eight classes of determiner:

– the indefinite article *a* or *an*. See p. 162.

> *A man came into the shop.*
> *An honest person would return the car to the owner.*

– the definite article *the*. See p. 164.

> *The dog chased the rabbit.*

– the demonstratives *this*, *that*, *these*, *those*. See p. 168.

> *This book is better than that one.*
> *These apples are redder than those ones.*

– the possessives *my*, *your*, *his*, *her*, *its*, *our*, *their*. See p. 209.

> *I gave my share to her sister.*
> *Shona found his book in her car.*

- the quantifiers *some, any, enough, no, all, both, half, double, several, much, many, more, most, few, fewer, fewest, a few, little* (meaning not much), *less, least, a little*. See pp. 171–177.

  > I've got *some* coffee but I haven't got *any* sugar.
  > Have you got *much* money on you?
  > There were *no* witnesses to the accident.
  > *Both* girls saw the attack.
  > *Few* people know the answer to that.
  > The safety net gives *little* help to those who need it most.

- the numbers, cardinal (*one, two, three...*), and ordinal (*first, second, third...*). See p. 176.

  > There's *one* thing I need to ask you.
  > The *two* boys grew up together in Manhattan.
  > *Three* men were found hiding in the building.
  > Their *second* child is due in October.
  > She lost in the *third* round of the tournament.

- the distributives *each, every, either, neither*. See p. 178.

  > *Each* child received a book.
  > *Every* girl was given a number to wear.
  > *Either* book should help you with the problem.

- the exclamatives *what, such*. See p. 180.

  > *What* nonsense!
  > *What* a shame!
  > They make *such* a fuss over small things!

Generally, a noun phrase has only one determiner in it, or none at all. See p. 160. A few determiners, e.g. *all, both*, and the numbers, can be used together with another determiner. See p. 160.

The indefinite article

The indefinite article is *a* or *an*. The form *an* is used before a word that starts with a vowel sound.

a girl   *a cat*
an eight-year-old girl   *an engineer*

The indefinite article is used with singular countable nouns:

– to refer to a person or a thing that you are mentioning for the first time in a conversation or a piece of writing.

> *A man was seen driving away in a black car.*

– to refer to a person or a thing which you do not want to be specific about.

> *I stopped off at a shop to buy a newspaper.*
> *You go past a petrol station on the left, and then you'll see our house on the right.*

– to refer to a person or a thing which you cannot be more specific about because there is not enough information.

> *A man called to see you this afternoon.*
> *There was a telephone call for you a minute ago.*

– in definitions.

> *An octopus is a sea creature with eight tentacles.*

– when you refer to a person's profession.

> *Her father is a dentist and her mother is a teacher.*

– to express a quantity, unless you wish to emphasize the number, when *one* must be used. The equivalent for plural nouns is *some* or no determiner at all. See p. 160.

> *I want a needle and a thimble.*
> *Would you like a glass of wine?*
> *There is only **one** glass of wine left in the bottle.*
> *Guy has bought a skateboard.*
> *We've got three pairs of rollerblades and one skateboard.*

It is the sound, not the spelling, that decides where *an* is used. For example, although *unique* begins with a vowel, the sound at the beginning resembles a *y*- sound.

> *an idiot*   *an awful mistake*
> *a unicorn*   *a unique experience*

> There are a few words that begin with a silent *h*-, in front of which *an* should be used. They are: *heir, heiress, honest, honour, hour.*

• Very formal or old-fashioned speakers also use the *an* form with some words beginning with an *h*- that is not silent, especially *historical* and *hotel*.

> *I waited an hour.*
> *They joined a historical society.*
> *They joined an historical society.*   (old-fashioned English)
> *They were staying at a hotel.*
> *They were staying at an hotel.*   (old-fashioned English)

The definite article

The definite article is *the*.

The definite article is used with singular and plural nouns. It is used both with countable nouns and uncountable nouns:

– to make definite or specific reference to a person or a thing that has already been referred to.

> *There's the man I was telling you about!*

– to refer to a person or thing that is already specific because of what those talking already know. In the first example below, *'the children'* would be members of our family and *'the swimming pool'* is the swimming pool we normally go to.

> *Let's take the children to the swimming pool.*
> *Did you switch the heating on?*
> *There were drinks in the fridge but the beer was soon finished.*

– to generalize about a whole class or species, usually of plants or animals. A singular noun is used for this purpose. The first example means *'The elephant species is hunted.'*

> *The elephant is still hunted for its tusks.*
> *The snowdrop is the first flower to arrive in the new year.*

– when it is followed by an adjective used as a noun indicating nationality or when generalizing about a whole class of people. *The Dutch* in the first example means *'Dutch people in general'.*

> *The Dutch are very skilful engineers.*
> *The poor were crowding the streets of the capital.*
> *The homeless were sheltered in the church.*

– before the names of rivers, groups of islands, seas, oceans, and mountain ranges.

> *The Thames*   *The Hebrides*
> *The North Sea*   *The Pacific*

– before the names of certain public institutions, most newspapers, and some magazines.

> *The British Museum*   *The Hilton Hotel*
> *The Lyceum Theatre*   *The Houses of Parliament*
> *The Independent*   *The Guardian*
> *The Listener*   *The New Scientist*

– before parts of the body when these are referred to in an impersonal way.

> *A stone struck him on the hand.*
> *Martin hit him on the head.*

• The definite article is rarely used with titles. Proper nouns that refer to persons, such as *Sue* and *Ron*, and proper nouns used in conjunction with titles, such as *Queen Elizabeth*, *Doctor Thomas*, and *Captain Parry*, only take a definite article if:

– they stand for the name of a thing such as a boat.

> *The Queen Elizabeth II is on a long cruise.*

– a distinction is being made between people who have identical names. This use can give emphasis to the noun.

> *Ah, no. The David Parry I know lives in Manchester.*
> *I saw Paul Kay in town this morning. – Not the Paul Kay?*

Nouns used without a determiner

Certain noun phrases do not have a determiner at all.

We usually leave out the determiner when we use a noun or a noun phrase in the plural to make a generalization.

> *He sells cars for a living.*
> *Tigers are nearing extinction.*
> *Onions are good for you.*
> *Grassy hills rise on all sides of the town.*

Singular nouns that are uncountable are used without a determiner when you are making a general reference.

> *New information is now available.*
> *Do you like jelly?*
> *This shop sells furniture.*

- This is particularly true when the uncountable noun is used for the first time in a general way in the course of a conversation or piece of writing. They can be used with a determiner when the reference becomes specific. For example, you can ask someone if they like *cake* as a rule, and then ask the person if she would like some of *your cake*.

> *The information she gave me was inaccurate.*
> *Would you like some of the jelly I made for the party?*
> *We don't let the dog climb onto the furniture.*

There are a number of idiomatic expressions that usually omit a determiner. Examples are expressions that refer to:

- travel, when you proceed *by: bicycle, car, bus, train, ship, boat, plane.*

> *Anna went by bicycle but Lucy went by car.*
> *He was chased by police on foot.*

– time with the prepositions *at, before,* or *by, dawn, sunrise, sunset, noon, midnight, night, supper, dinner, day, night.*

> *Catherine rose at dawn and went to bed at sunset.*
> *We swam in the pool by day and partied by night.*

– meals: to have *breakfast, tea, lunch.*

> *Jane had breakfast at home.*
> *She met Diana for lunch.*

– institutions, with the prepositions *to* or *at: church, hospital, prison, school, work.*

> *John was taken to hospital with a broken ankle.*
> *Lucy has been kept late at school today.*
> *Ruth was at home all day.*

– seasons of the year, when you are generalizing, e.g: *in spring, in summer, in autumn, in winter.*

> *In autumn, the grapes are harvested by hand.*
> *The place is packed in summer.*

However, all of these words are used with the definite article when you are talking about a specific time, place, season, etc.

> *Philip travelled by the same train as Mehandra.*
> *Just look at the wonderful sunset.*
> *Pam works at the hospital.*
> *I can't work well in the summer.*

Demonstratives

Demonstratives are used to specify the distance of something in space or time in relation to the speaker.

The **demonstratives** are: *this*, *that*, *these*, *those*.

This and *these* refer to objects near the speaker.

>*This apple looks ripe.*
>*These apples come from Australia.*

The reference may be nearness in time, especially future time.

>*I'll call round this afternoon.*
>*The festival ends this Thursday.*
>*This summer is the warmest I can remember.*

That and *those* refer to objects that are further away from the speaker.

>*I think that boy over there is lost.*
>*Can you see those people up on the hill?*

This and *that* are used before singular countable nouns and uncountable nouns.

>*I can touch this picture, but I can't reach that one.*
>*This book is mine, but that magazine isn't.*

These and *those* are used before plural countable nouns.

>*I'm peeling these potatoes for a shepherd's pie.*
>*Those men are mending the roof.*

Possessives

Possessives are used to specify the ownership of an item, or, if the noun refers to something animate, to specify a relationship.

> *That is my car.*
> *Mr Smith was my teacher in the sixth form.*

The form of the possessive changes according to the number and gender of the person or thing that possesses the item.

> *His brothers all came to the wedding.*
> *Their aunt lives in London, but their cousins live in Berlin.*
> *Your shoes are under your bed.*

person	singular	plural
1st	my	our
2nd	your	your
3rd (masculine)	his	their
3rd (feminine)	her	their
3rd (neuter)	its	their

Possessive determiners, which can go into a noun phrase, are not the same as possessive pronouns (*mine, hers, yours*, etc.), which can stand alone.
See p. 144.

Another sort of possessive is the **possessive phrase**.

This acts just like a possessive word but is a noun or noun phrase ending in -'s or -s'. A possessive phrase acts as a possessive determiner, but may itself include one of the other determiners.

Robert's mother
the visitors' washroom
a good day's work
the Prime Minister's press secretary

Sally's new job
the residents' dining room
my wife's cousin

Quantifiers

Quantifiers are used to indicate the amount or quantity of something referred to by a noun. They are different from numbers because they indicate an approximate amount rather than an exact amount. They can be grouped according to their use.

all, some, any, much, enough, no

– You can use *all*, *some*, *any*, or *enough*, before a plural countable noun or an uncountable noun.

> *Can I have some chips, please?*
> *Anna gave me all her money.*
> *Peter never has any time to visit us.*

You can use *no* before a singular or a plural countable noun or an uncountable noun.

> *There were no pictures of the party.*
> *There is no hospital in this town.*
> *No information has been released yet.*

– *Some, any, much,* and *enough* are used to refer to a part of the item.

> *Would you like some ice cream?*
> *We didn't have much success.*
> *I haven't seen enough evidence to convince me.*
> *I couldn't find any fresh milk at the shop.*

All and *no* refer to the whole of the item.

> *All the milk has been used.*
> *There is no milk in the fridge.*

– *Some* is used in positive sentences.

> *I've bought some chocolate.*
> *I saw some lovely shoes in town this morning.*

– *Any* is used in negative sentences.

> *I didn't buy any chocolate this week.*
> *I haven't seen any birds in the garden today.*

• In questions, *any* is used when there is no particular expectation about the answer; *some* is used when the answer is expected to be positive.

> *Have you got any fresh bread?*
> *Has Paul heard any news about the accident?*
> *Would you like some cake, Aisha?*

• The use of *no* with *there is/are* is very common.

> *There was no post today.*
> *There are no jobs available for electricians at the moment.*

half, double, both

– *Half* can be used with countable nouns and with uncountable nouns.

> *Half the time I didn't understand what was going on.*
> *Half the students came from overseas.*

– *Double* is used with uncountable nouns.

> *We're going to need double the present supply of water.*
> *They want double the money they originally asked for.*

– *Both* is used to define two things represented by a plural countable noun.

> *Both men were given another chance.*
> *Both dogs had to be put down.*

See p. 161 for more information about quantifiers when they are used with other determiners.

The following quantifiers are used to express **graded** amounts of an item (e.g. whether there is more or less of something).

> *Have you seen many tourists in town?*
> *Yes, I've seen more tourists than usual.*
> *I think most tourists just stay for a couple of days.*

> *I didn't put much petrol in the car.*
> *I think we need more petrol.*
> *The news caused much excitement.*
> *Most information about our services is available on the Internet.*

– *Many, more, most* are used with graded quantities of plural countable nouns.

> *Have you seen many tourists in town?*
> *Yes, I've seen more tourists than usual.*
> *I think most tourists just stay for a couple of days.*

– *Much, more, most* are used with graded quantities of uncountable nouns.

> *I didn't put much petrol in the car.*
> *I think we need more petrol.*
> *The news caused much excitement.*
> *Most information about our services is available on the Internet.*

– *Few*, *fewer*, *fewest* are used with graded quantities of plural countable nouns.

> *Few people know the answer to this problem.*
> *Fewer loans are being granted than usual.*
> *Japanese workers take the fewest holidays.*

– *Little*, *less*, *least* are used with graded quantities of uncountable nouns.

> *There is little chance of rain today.*
> *This technique causes less harm to the environment.*
> *I need to get from one place to another with the least inconvenience.*

• *A few*, and *a little* are different from *few* and *little* on their own because they have a positive sense. *Few* means 'not many',

> *Few buildings survived the earthquake.*

but *a few* means 'several'.

> *A few kind people helped the injured man.*
> *A few delays are inevitable.*

Little means 'not much',

> *The students were given very little help with their projects.*
> *Edward got little encouragement from his parents.*

but *a little* means 'some'.

> *I need a little help from my friends.*
> *Everyone needs a little encouragement now and then.*
> *Do you take sugar? – Just a little, please.*

Few and *little* are often used in a negative sense to suggest disappointment or pessimism, while *a few* and *a little* are used in a positive sense to suggest that things are better than they might have been.

Numbers

There are two common kinds of number:

Cardinal numbers are used in all forms of counting that involve a total.

> *one* chair   *two* chairs
> *a hundred* people   *ten thousand* pounds

Ordinal numbers are used to talk about where something is placed in an ordered sequence. They are often used right after the definite article or after a possessive.

> *The first horse in was disqualified.*
> *He's celebrating his fifty-first birthday in August.*
> *The company has just celebrated its one hundred and fiftieth anniversay.*

Ordinals are mostly formed by adding *-th* to a cardinal number.

> *fourth*   *twentieth*   *hundredth*
> *fifth*   *forty-ninth*   *millionth*
> *sixth*   *eighty-sixth*   *thousandth*
> *nine hundred and ninety ninth*

Some examples of exceptions are the words *first*, *second*, and *third*, and combinations which contain them, such as *twenty-first*.

Cardinal numbers can be used at the beginning of a noun phrase, like determiners.

> *one* chair   *two* chairs
> *a hundred* people   *ten thousand* pounds

or on their own, like pronouns.

> *And then there were three.*
> *Four of them came towards us.*
> *The other two went to get help.*

- Grammatically speaking, the words *next*, *last*, and *another* can also be regarded as ordinal numbers.

> *It rained on last day of our holiday.*
> *The next horse in was declared the winner.*
> *Oh no, not another birthday!*

Ordinal numbers and the words *next* and *last* are sometimes called **postdeterminers**, since they come after the word *the* or a possessive .

> *The next three days are going to be very exciting.*
> *The last three years have been difficult for everyone.*
> *We have to get off the bus at the next stop.*

- An ordinal, as well as *next*, *last*, and *another*, can be used together with a cardinal number in the same noun phrase.

> *The first three correct entries will win a prize.*
> *He scored another three goals before the end of the match.*

- To show that a cardinal number is only approximate, the word, *some* is often used before it.

> *Some two hundred people gathered in the pouring rain.*

Distributives

Distributives are determiners that are used to talk about how something is shared out or divided.

The distributives are *each*, *every*, *either*, and *neither*. They are used with a singular noun.

> *Each child was given a balloon.*
> *I remember every detail of our conversation.*
> *Either child could win the prize.*
> *Neither plan was successful.*

— *Each* and *every* are not used with proper nouns.

— *Each* is used to refer to separate persons or things in a group of two or more.

> *Four girls came and each one sang a song.*
> *Each ticket should have a number on the back.*

— *Every* is used to refer to all the persons or things in a group of three or more.

> *Every teacher has a key to the building.*
> *Katrina danced with every boy at the party.*

— *Every* can be used in front of ordinal numbers. '*Every second house*' means *the second house, the fourth house, the sixth house*, and so on.

> *I have to work every third weekend.*
> *Every fourth house has a garage.*

- *Either* is used to talk about one of two people or things.

   They did not appoint either man as captain.
   Either restaurant would suit me.

- *Neither* is used to exclude both of two people or things that are being referred to.

   They appointed neither man as captain.
   Neither restaurant is cheap enough.

Exclamatives

Exclamatives are used to introduce an exclamation of surprise, admiration, or a similar emotion.

The exclamatives are: *what, such*.

Exclamations introduced by one of these words consist either of:

– the exclamative in a noun phrase alone (usually with *What...*).

> *What a laugh!*
> *What awful weather!*

– the exclamative and its noun phrase in a complete clause.

> *He is such a nice man!*
> *You always wear such lovely things!*
> *What a pleasant surprise this is!*

Noun phrases with several determiners

Most noun phrases contain only one determiner or none at all, but if there are more, they follow a definite order. Determiners can be divided into four groups, depending on what other determiners they can be used with and the order that they follow.

There are two large groups:

A *the, this, these, that, those, a(n),* and the possessives *my, your, her, his,* etc.

> *a ripe orange*   *my young sister*
> *this ripe orange*   *our young sister*

B *another, some, any, no, either, neither, each, enough, a few, a little.*

> *each ripe orange*   *another sister*
> *some ripe oranges*   *enough money*

The words in groups A and B are known as the **central determiners**. A noun phrase will normally contain only one central determiner.

• The group A and group B words cannot be used together, with the exception that words in group B may be followed by a group A word if *of* is placed between them.

> *some* of *those oranges*   *neither* of *my sisters*

• Words in group A can be used in combination with determiners in groups C and D (below).

> *Both girls were reading.*
> *Both my young sisters are really naughty.*
> *All visitors must now leave the ship.*
> *All the visitors left the ship.*

There are two smaller groups.

C The smallest group consists of the words: *all, both, half, double,* and *twice*. These can be used on their own before a noun or before the group A determiners above. Some speakers of English prefer to insert *of* between *all, both,* or *half* and a central determiner.

> *All of the visitors left the ship.*
> *Half of the oranges will have to be thrown away.*

• The words in group C are sometimes called **predeterminers**. The exclamatives *such* and *what* belong to this group. See p. 180 for more details about these.

D The words in the fourth group are, *every, many, several, few, little, much, more, most, less,* the ordinal numbers *first, second, third* etc., and *last*. These can be used on their own before a noun,

> *Every move was carefully recorded.*
> *She did many kind things.*
> *She has few friends.*
> *Last orders, please.*

or after the A group of determiners.

> *Your every move is being watched.*
> *The many kind things she did went unnoticed.*
> *Her few possessions had been stolen.*
> *The first thing she did was call her mother.*
> *I would rather forget these last few days.*

Adjectives

Adjectives are used with nouns to make the meaning more specific. If you use the noun *'bear'* it can mean any animal of that species. As soon as you say *'a large, brown bear'* you have given two of its **attributes** (colour and size). A noun is said to be **modified** by its adjectives.

Adjectives have two main features:

– Most adjectives can go before a noun; this is known as their **attributive** use.

> *a tall girl*
> *green grass*
> *four badly behaved little boys*

– Most adjectives can also go after a link verb such as *be* or *seem*; this is known as their **predicative** use.

> *The roses are yellow.*
> *The girls are getting tall.*
> *These books seem really interesting.*

Any word that can go into both of these positions is a normal adjective. When used predicatively (after a link verb), an adjective can either describe the **subject** of a sentence,

> *The roses are yellow.*
> *The girls are getting tall.*
> *These books are really interesting.*

or the **object** of the sentence. See also p. 11.

> *Anna painted the room green.*
> *The children drove him mad.*

Adjective order

The order is normally:

– adjectives that describe feelings or qualities.

> *pleasant* childhood memories
> *beautiful* brown hands

– adjectives of size, age, temperature, or measurement.

> some *hot* scones
> a *rectangular* pie dish
> those *nice young* girls
> a *lovely big* smile

– adjectives of colour.

> the *green* hills of home
> smart *brown* shoes
> her beautiful *blue* eyes

– adjectives of nationality or origin.

> those friendly *Spanish* girls
> both the small grey *Irish* horses
> an elegant *French* woman

– adjectives denoting the substance or material that something is made from.

> a large *wooden* door
> an elegant *silver* teapot

It is possible to pile up adjectives in English, but in practice more than four is uncommon.

> *a happy young blonde German girl*
> *beautiful old English half-timbered houses*

- Adjectives before a noun are not usually separated by *and*, unless they are adjectives of colour.

> *a green and white striped shirt*
> *a red and blue flag*

- Adjectives can themselves be premodified by adverbs of degree. See also p. 186.

> *an* extremely *intelligent student*
> *a* very *tall man*
> *a* fairly *untidy flat*

Some adjectives can only be used predicatively (i.e. after a link verb such as *be*). Many of the members of this group begin with *a-*:

> *afloat, afraid, alike, alive, alone, ashamed, asleep, awake.*

> *Our balloon was aloft at last.*
> *Charles is abroad again.*
> *The child is afraid.*
> *The girls were asleep and were not aware of the noise.*

When an adjective is used predicatively it may have to be followed by a particular preposition if the phrase continues.

> *She was glad.*   *She was glad to help.*
> *He was afraid.*   *He was afraid for his life.*
> *I was free.*   *I was free from guilt.*
> *It is devoid of interest.*   *He was intent on revenge.*

There are some adjectives such as *devoid (of)*, *intent (on)* that always have to have a following phrase.

Although attributive adjectives usually come before the noun that they modify, there are some that can go immediately after the noun, particularly when they are used with plural nouns, e.g. *absent, present, involved, concerned*. When these adjectives are used in this position they may have a different meaning from the one that they have when they come before the noun.

> *Everyone present was given tea.*
> *The present government took over four years ago.*
> *The people absent from work were all ill.*
> *Let us toast absent friends.*
> *The dealers concerned were sent to jail.*
> *There were letters from concerned parents.*

- There are some set phrases which always have an adjective immediately after the noun.

> *the Princess Royal*   *a lion rampant*
> *the president elect*   *the Attorney General*

Premodifiers and postmodifiers

Adjectives, determiners, and other nouns can all be used to describe a noun more specifically; that is, they can be used as **modifiers**. Nouns can also be modified by prepositional groups (groups of words that begin with a preposition) and relative clauses added after the noun. See p. 270 for more about relative clauses.

To make it simpler to talk about any modifying word which comes in front of a noun, we can use the term **premodifier**.

> *a young man*   *these onions*
> *my aunt's house*   *the elephant house*

Those modifiers that come after the noun are called **postmodifiers**.

> *the young man with the guitar*
> *the person who met me*
> *the girl I was standing near*
> *the people involved*

Comparison

The **comparative** form of an adjective is commonly used to compare two people, things, or states, when you want to say that one thing has a larger or smaller amount of a quality than another.

- If the second part of the comparison is mentioned it follows *than*.

    Anna is taller than Mary but Mary is older.
    Emma is much slimmer than when I last saw her.
    Online learning is less expensive than conventional college
        courses.

- Comparison in which you are considering whether two people or things are equal is shown by using *as…as* in the affirmative and *not as…as* or *not so…as* in the negative.

    Helen is as tall as Linda, but not as strong.

The **superlative** form is used for more than two people, things, or states, when one thing has qualities that exceed all the others. Superlative adjectives have *the* in front of them, but it can be omitted in predicative positions.

    That is the smallest camera I have ever seen.
    He gave the least expensive gift to his sister.
    I'll have whichever is (the) ripest.

There are two ways in which the comparative and superlative forms of adjectives are formed:

- You add *-er* (comparative) or *-est* (superlative) to the adjective. Adjectives with one syllable usually take these endings.

	comparative	superlative
bright	brighter	the brightest
long	longer	the longest
sharp	sharper	the sharpest

- If the word already ends in -e, the -e must be left off. If a word ends in -y, it usually takes -er or -est, and the -y changes to -i.

	comparative	superlative
wise	wiser	the wisest
pretty	prettier	the prettiest
weary	wearier	the weariest

- You add the word more or most in front of the adjective. Adjectives with three syllables or more use more or most in front of the adjective.

	comparative	superlative
fortunate	more fortunate	the most fortunate
relevant	more relevant	the most relevant

Adjectives formed from participles use more or most as well.

	comparative	superlative
provoking	more provoking	the most provoking
enthralled	more enthralled	the most enthralled

To indicate the opposite of both the -er/-est and the more/most forms of comparison, less or least is always used.

	comparative	superlative
sharp	less sharp	the least sharp
fortunate	less fortunate	the least fortunate
interesting	less interesting	the least interesting
involved	less involved	the least involved

Adjectives with two syllables (including those that already end in -er) can follow either pattern or sometimes both patterns. If you are doubtful about a two-syllable adjective, use the *more/most* pattern.

	comparative	superlative
shallow or	shallower more shallow	the shallowest the most shallow
polite or	politer more polite	the politest the most polite

A small group of irregular adjectives have quite different forms for the comparative and superlative forms.

	comparative	superlative
good	better	the best
bad	worse	the worst
far	further	the furthest

Adverbs and adverbials

When you want to add information about *how, when, where,* or *to what extent* something has happened, you can use an **adverbial**. Many adverbials are members of the group of words called **adverbs**, but adverbials are not necessarily just single words. They can also be word groups, prepositional phrases, or even clauses. They are sometimes called **adjuncts**.

Adverbials generally modify the meaning of a verb,

> I *greatly* admire your courage.
> They changed *hurriedly* into their pyjamas.
> Monica hummed *softly* as she washed the car.
> The firework exploded *with a loud bang.*
> He ran *across the lawn* towards the house.

an adjective,

> Harry is *absolutely* terrified of flying.
> You must admit that he can be *rather* boring.
> That is *quite* silly.
> Fears like that are *very* real to the sufferer.

another adverb,

> I thought about it *quite* seriously.
> The children are behaving *remarkably* well.
> Ali objected *very* strongly to the plan.

a whole sentence,

> *Frankly,* I think he is lying.
> *Nevertheless,* we must give him a chance.
> *Honestly,* I didn't mean to be rude to you.

or a prepositional phrase.

> *We are really in a no-win situation.*

Most adverbials are optional parts of a clause or phrase, but there are a few verbs that need an adverb to complete their meaning. See p. 81. Conditional sentences must also have an adverbial clause, usually one beginnining with *if* or *unless*. See p. 267 for more about adverbial clauses.

Adverbials can be divided into:

– adverbials of **manner**, which express *how*: e.g. *slowly, with care, well*.

> *Two men were working their way slowly up the hillside.*

– adverbials of **place**, which express *where*: e.g. *there, here, up, in town*.

> *Two men were working their way up the hillside.*

– adverbials of **time**, which express *when*: e.g. *now, today, last night, lately*.

> *Two men were lost on the hills yesterday.*

– adverbials of **degree**, which express *to what extent*: e.g. *largely, extremely, much, by a whisker*.

> *It was largely their own fault.*

– adverbials of **frequency**, which express *how often*: e.g. *rarely, often, sometimes, twice daily*.

> *Search parties went out every hour.*

Although adverbials change the meaning of clauses or phrases, they are usually optional parts of the group or clause.

> *He coughed nervously.*
> *Really, I think you are mistaken.*
> *In a fit of temper, he slammed the door shut.*

They stand outside the word, group, or clause that they are associated with. For example, the same adverb can in one sentence be part of the description of a verb, while in another sentence, it may modify the whole clause.

> *I think she acted honestly.*
> *Honestly, who does she think she is?*

The exceptions are that:

– Some verbs must be followed by an adverbial to complete their meaning.

> *Alice behaved wonderfully.*
> *Sylvia acted unlawfully.*
> *Justin sped down the corridor.*

– Some verbs require both an object and an adverbial to complete their meaning. See also p. 28.

> *Ranjit put the folder back.*
> *James stood the golf clubs in the corner.*
> *Clare placed the cover over the cot.*

• New meanings can be made by combining an adverbial with a verb to make a phrasal verb. See also p. 81 for more about phrasal verbs.

> *The car pulled out.*
> *Lydia went away.*
> *Things are looking up.*

Adverbials are classified according to the way they modify a word, group or clause. In addition to the uses given on p. 191, one important use of a special group of adverbials is to show how a sentence relates to what comes before it. An adverb used in this way is called a **sentence adverb**.

> *Nevertheless, we must give him an answer.*
> *However, it's good advice.*
> *On the other hand, we cannot turn him down.*

Another use of adverbials is to let your listener or reader know your point of view about a situation. This is called a **viewpoint adverb**.

> *Foolishly, I gave him my address.*
> *Clearly, he deserves our help.*
> *Actually, I don't mind.*

A further group of adverbials, all of them adverbs of degree, can only be used with adjectives or other adverbs. Examples are *very, rather, quite, really, too, somewhat*. These are sometimes called **submodifiers** because they can weaken or strengthen the descriptive value of the adjective.

> *She seems rather nice.*
> *Angus is a very good tennis player.*
> *Kim gave me this really expensive bag.*

They are used mainly with adjectives of quality. An adverb can also be submodified by another adverb.

> *She began to cry, quite loudly.*
> *Sometimes I think you're too easily impressed.*
> *It must have been done extremely recently.*
> *The car was almost totally submerged in the flood water.*

There are certain adverbs (and adverbials) which can only be used with verbs and so cannot modify adjectives.

- Most adverbs are able to come:

- before the verb phrase or the subject

     Happily she ran over the sand dunes.
     Tearfully, he told his brother the whole story.

- after the verb phrase or the object

     She ran happily over the sand dunes.
     He was telling the whole story tearfully to his brother.

- between the auxiliary and the main verb.

     She was happily running about over the sand dunes.
     He was tearfully telling the whole story to his brother.

- Some adverbs can only come **after** the verb, e.g. *back, up, down, sideways, clockwise.*

     Suddenly the frightened animal ran back.
     They hammered the wedge in sideways.

- A few adverbs can come **before** the main verb, e.g. *barely, hardly, little, rarely, scarcely, seldom.*

     Scarcely had she spoken when it came crashing down.
     He had hardly eaten anything.
     Seldom have I seen such ridiculous behaviour.

A subordinate clause that begins with one of these words adopts the same word order as a question. These are called **broad negatives**, because they give a negative meaning to a clause.

Compare:

They never noticed her presence.
They scarcely noticed her presence.

> Some speakers take care not to place an adverb between
> the *to* and the **base form** of the verb in a *'to* **infinitive**'.
> This is called a 'split infinitive'. There is no good reason to
> regard a split infinitive as an error; the choice is a matter
> of personal preference.
>
> > *I need to really think hard about this.*
> > *I really need to think hard about this.*

Adverbs with nouns and pronouns

While **adverbs** can modify most parts of speech, they normally do
not modify **nouns** or **pronouns**. Much more common is the use of
an adverb of degree to modify a whole **noun phrase**.

> *Dominic thought that Geoffrey was rather a good teacher.*
> *Jason is quite a skilled craftsman.*

There is a small group of adverbs that can modify nouns and indefinite
pronouns.

> *the man downstairs*
> *the example above*
> *Almost everyone brought a bottle to the party.*

Form of adverbs

Most **adverbs** are formed by adding -ly to the end of the related adjective.

slow	*slowly*
clever	*cleverly*
annual	*annually*

Exceptionally, words which end in -*ble* drop off the -*e* before -*ly* is added. So do the words *true* and *due*.

sensible	*sensibly*
suitable	*suitably*
true	*truly*
due	*duly*

A common spelling mistake is to add -*ley*. This mistake is often made when the adjective ends in the letter -*e*. Note the correct spelling of adverbs formed from adjectives ending in -*e*.

extreme	*extremely*
divine	*divinely*
free	*freely*

Adjectives that end in -*y* change to -*i* before adding -*ly*, unless, like *sly* or *dry*, they have only one syllable.

happy	*happily*
greedy	*greedily*
sly	*slyly*

Some adverbs keep the same spelling as the adjective to which they are related. It is often difficult to tell at first whether the word is an adjective or an adverb. The general rule is to look at the other words which it occurs with. If it comes before a noun it is probably an adjective.

> *a short way*   *a late meeting*
> *a long pause*   *an early lecture*

If it relates to a verb or an adjective it is probably an adverb.

> *The lesson was cut short.*
> *We met late at night.*
> *Don't stay long.*
> *He came in early.*

Some adverbs have the same spelling as a preposition. They can be told apart if you look at the words they are found with. Prepositions are normally used in front of noun phrases, because prepositions must have an object.

> *He rushed in an attempt to catch his bus.*
> *She hurried over her meal because she was late.*

When the word is found without an object, especially at the end of a clause, it will usually be an adverb.

> *He rushed in.*
> *She hurried over.*

Just like certain adjectives, some adverbs have comparative and superlative forms and can be used with submodifiers.

Kim treated Sharon *well*, Karen *less well* and Janice
   the least well.
Malcolm walked *the most slowly* of all of them.
Tariq acted *very kindly* towards him.
You must behave *far more sensibly* in future.
This graph shows that girls performed *the best* at maths
   this year.

Superlative forms of adverbs are quite rare.

Pronouns

A **pronoun** is a word that is used in the place of a noun or a whole noun phrase.

Pronouns are commonly used:

– in place of a noun or a noun phrase that has already been mentioned, when the repetition of the noun or noun phrase would be very strange.

> *Sam has to go to the airport. Can you give **him** a lift?*
> *The young prince and his wife came out on to the balcony.*
>   ***They** waved to the crowd.*
> *The mechanic tested the starter motor. **It** would not work.*
>   ***He** tried **it** again.*

– when we know perfectly well who or what is referred to. When, for example, I use the pronoun *I* it is because it would be unusual to refer to myself by name.

> *I'm sorry I'm late.*
> *We'd better ring and say **we're** not coming.*

– when the name of someone or something is not known.

> ***He's** the man who came to the house yesterday!*
> *Who's she?*

Types of pronoun

There are seven different types of pronoun, classified according to their meaning and use.

The **personal** pronouns can be used as subject or object in a clause.

> *He gave her a box of chocolates.*
> *We saw them both on Friday.*
> *I can see you!*

The **reflexive** pronouns are used in object position when the action of a verb is performed on the subject by the subject. They are obligatory with certain verbs.

> *The puppy entangled itself in the lead.*
> *I've just cut myself on a piece of glass.*

Reflexive pronouns are also used for emphasis.

> *Never mind. I'll do it myself.*
> *The professor himself did not know the answer.*

The **possessive** pronouns indicate ownership.

> *Give it back, it's mine.*
> *Perhaps it really is theirs after all.*

The **demonstrative** pronouns indicate items that are near to or far from us.

> *This is Betty's and that is Peter's.*
> *These are nice. Where did you find them?*

The **relative** pronouns are used to link a modifying clause to a noun phrase or to a clause.

> *I don't know what you mean.*
> *That's the girl who always comes top.*

The **interrogative** pronouns are used to ask a question about the noun phrase they stand in for.

> *What would you like for lunch?*
> *Which is the fresh milk?*
> *Who was responsible?*

The **indefinite** pronouns are used for a broad range of reference when it is not necessary or not possible to use a personal pronoun.

> *Everyone had a compass and a whistle.*
> *Neither wanted to give in and apologize.*
> *Much needs to be done.*

Personal pronouns

Personal pronouns are used as the subject, object, or complement in a clause. They are commonly found taking the place of a noun phrase when it is mentioned for a second time.

person	subject	singular object	subject	plural object
1st	I	me	we	us
2nd	you	you	you	you
3rd masculine	he	him	they	them
3rd feminine	she	her	they	them
3rd neutral	it	it	they	them

We use the 1st person pronoun *I* to take the role of the speaker. The 2nd person pronoun *you* is used to take the role of the listener. In the case of *you*, there is only one pronoun to cover the singular and the plural, so that it is sometimes necessary to use a form of words that will make clear who is being addressed.

> *You should be ashamed.*
> *All of you should be ashamed.*
> *You must all stop writing now.*

When more than one personal pronoun is used with a verb, the order is normally: 3rd or 2nd person before 1st person; 2nd person before 3rd person.

> *She and I do not get on very well.*
> *You and he should buy the boat between you.*

When two pronouns or a personal noun and a personal
pronoun are the joint subject of a verb, the subject form
of the pronouns must be used. Avoid the common
mistake of saying, for example, *Jerry and me are...*

Jerry and I are going to paint the house ourselves.
He and I are going to paint it.
Melanie and I are going shopping.

When either two pronouns or a noun plus a personal pronoun are the
joint object of a verb, the object form of the pronoun must be used:

They decided to help Jane and me.

The object form of a pronoun is used after a preposition.
Avoid the common mistake of saying, for example,
between you and I.

Between you and me, I don't like this place.
Wasn't that kind of me?

The object form is usual in everyday spoken usage. In formal and old-
fashioned English, the subject form is used:

– after the verb *be*.

It's me.	Informal
It is I.	Formal/old-fashioned
I saw at once that it was her.	Informal
I saw at once that it was she.	Formal/old-fashioned

– after *than* in comparison with *be*.

John is smaller than him.	Informal
John is smaller than he (is).	Formal/old-fashioned
Sylvia is cleverer than me.	Informal
Sylvia is cleverer than I (am).	Formal/old-fashioned

Otherwise, *than* + **object** pronoun is necessary.

She's probably done more than me.

• The object form is also used to supply short answers to questions.

Who found Gran's watch? – Me. Aren't I clever!

Reflexive pronouns

Reflexive pronouns are used:

person	singular	plural
1st	myself	ourselves
2nd	yourself	yourselves
3rd masculine	himself	themselves
3rd feminine	herself	themselves
3rd neuter	itself	themselves
General	oneself	

– when the speaker or writer is referring to an action that he or she has caused to happen and of which he or she is also the object.

> *I cut myself with the carving knife.*
> *Sometimes I just don't like myself very much.*

– when the direct object or prepositional object of a sentence has the same reference as the subject.

> *John looked at her.*
> *John looked at himself.*
> *John taught himself to play the guitar.*

The reflexive form *oneself* can be used to refer to people in general.

> *The first golden rule is not to take oneself too seriously.*

It can also be used as a substitute for the 1st person singular. If it is used like this, the subject pronoun should be *one*. In normal direct speech this usage is often felt to be rather pretentious.

> *One asks oneself whether it is worth the bother.*
> *One owes it to oneself to do something worthwhile.*

Some verbs take a reflexive pronoun only in particular uses of the verb.

>   *Jeremy introduced himself.*
>   *The cat washed itself.*

The reflexive pronoun can be left out if it is obvious that the subject was performing the action of the verb on him- or herself.

>   *Jeremy washed and dressed, then went out.*

When a preposition is followed by a pronoun, the pronoun is normally in the object form.

>   *They all looked at him in silence.*

If that pronoun refers to the subject of the main verb, however, it must be a reflexive pronoun.

>   *She looked at herself in the mirror.*

- The reflexive can be used to make something you say stronger. To make a strong point, we sometimes use a normal subject or object pronoun and a reflexive pronoun as well.

>   *He told me himself that he was leaving.*
>   *I'll do it myself.*

- The reflexive can also be used with or without *by* meaning 'alone' or 'without help'.

>   *I think you should try and do it yourself.*
>   *Did she do that all by herself?*

The compound pronouns *each other* and *one another* are not true reflexives. They are used when two or more subjects mutually take part in an action. They are sometimes called **reciprocals**.

> *They should stop blaming one another.*
> *We will always love each other.*

Possessive pronouns

Possessive pronouns are used when you want to indicate who owns or is associated with an item.

> All those books are **hers**.
> Those suitcases are **ours**.
> Are you selling those books? I'd never sell any **of mine**.
> Those awful cousins **of yours** are here.
> This TV is really cheap. – Yes, **ours** was a bit more expensive,
>   but better quality.

There are separate forms for the singular and the plural except in the 2nd person. In the 3rd person singular the form changes to match the gender of the possessor.

> I'm looking for Helen's trainers. Perhaps these are **hers**.
> These are our seats and the ones in front are **yours**.

possessive determiner	possessive pronoun
my	mine
your (singular)	yours
his	his
her	hers
its	(no form)
our	ours
your (plural)	yours
their	theirs

Note that none of these words should be spelled with an apostrophe. Avoid the common mistake of writing it's for the possessive form. It's is a short form for it is.

The demonstrative pronouns

The **demonstrative pronouns** are used instead of a noun phrase to indicate distance in time or space in relation to the speaker. They also indicate grammatical number – singular or plural.

	singular	plural
near	this	these
far	that	those

- Note that the demonstrative pronouns have the same spelling as demonstrative determiners. See also p. 160. Usually a demonstrative pronoun substitutes for a noun phrase that contains the same word being used as a determiner.

  Would you like to share some of this pizza with me?
  Would you like to share this with me?
  I'd like you to put these things away before we go.
  I'd like you to put these away before we go.

- It is regarded as impolite to use a demonstrative pronoun to refer directly to a person, except when making introductions.

  John, this is Harry Forbes, my colleague.
  This is my husband, Rob.
  Mum, this is my form teacher, Miss Evans.

Relative pronouns

The relative pronouns are the words *who*, *whom*, *which*, and *that*.

	person	thing
subject	*who* or *that*	*which* or *that*
object	*whom* or *that*	*which* or *that*
possessive	*whose*	*whose*

The function of a relative pronoun is to link a subordinate clause to a main clause.

> He might lose his job, *which would be disastrous.*
> *She promised* to give away all the money, *which was a bit rash.*

A subordinate clause introduced by a relative pronoun is called a **relative clause**.

Relative pronouns refer back to a noun phrase or pronoun that has just been mentioned. All relative pronouns must come as near as possible to the start of the clause that they are in. The only words that normally come before them in the clause are prepositions or conjunctions.

The choice of relative pronoun is influenced as follows:

– *That* as a relative pronoun never has a preposition before it.

> *That is* a kind thought, *for which I am most grateful.*
> *This is* the person *that Annie was talking about.*
> *This is* the person *about whom Annie was talking.*

- *Which* is not used for human subjects or objects.

  > *That is* the car *which she has just bought.*
  > *I have found* a ring *which you will love.*

- *Who* and *whom* are restricted to human subjects or objects.

  > *He introduced me to* his friend, *who had just returned from China.*
  > *I liked* the actor *who was playing Oedipus.*

- In **defining** relative clauses (see p. 270), *that* can be used instead of *which* and is sometimes used instead of *who* or *whom*.

  > *I have found* a ring *which you will love.*
  > *I have found* a ring *that you will love.*
  > *She is* the girl *who was at Sam's party.*
  > *She is* the girl *that was at Sam's party.*

The **object** form of the relative pronoun is used as the object of a verb or a preposition, but because *whom* is very formal, it is not often used: in everyday English, *who* is usually used instead.

  > *The late Principal of the College, whom we all remember with
  > affection, left this bursary in her will.*

  > *I discovered who he was visiting.*   neutral
  > *I discovered whom he was visiting.*   formal

- In informal writing and speech, any **preposition** is placed after the verb phrase instead of before the relative pronoun.

  > *The girl who Brian was talking to seemed nervous.*
  > *The people who he had been working for that summer had
  > offered him a permanent job.*

- In informal and spoken English, a defining relative pronoun referring to the object of the clause may be left out entirely.

    *He is the **person** (that/who/whom) Annie was talking about.*
    *That is the **car** (which/that) she has just bought.*

Interrogative pronouns

The **interrogative pronouns** *who*, *whom*, and *whose* are used only for reference to people. The interrogative pronouns *which* and *what* are used for reference to things.

	subject	object	possessive
people	who	whom	whose
things	which what	which what	

Interrogative pronouns allow us to build a question around the thing that the pronoun refers to. See p. 237, where they are explained more generally under the heading of **WH-** words.

> *Who is dancing with Lucy?*
> *Which of these books would you recommend?*
> *What do you do when you're on holiday?*
> *Whose are these clothes?*

Who is used to ask questions about people in general.

> *Who is that man over there?*
> *Who did this?*
> *Who controls the day-to-day running of the business?*

What is used to ask questions about things in general when the answer is an open one. *What* can be either a subject or an object in a clause.

> *What happened next?*
> *What did you have for lunch?*

Which is used ask for identification of a particular person or a particular thing in a group.

> *Which do you prefer, working in theatre or film?*
> *Which is your favourite Simpsons episode?*

Whose is the possessive form of the pronoun. It is used when a person is the possessor.

> *Whose is that sports car outside?*
> *Whose side are you on?*

- *Whom* is the object form of *who*. It is a very formal word and one which most speakers avoid using in casual conversation, when *who* could be used instead. When writing, however, it is usual to use *whom*.

> Informal
> *Who do you have in mind?*
> *Who were you speaking to?*
>
> Formal
> *Whom have you in mind?*
> *To whom were you speaking?*

- The object forms of the interrogative pronoun are used after a preposition. In informal and everyday usage, you can place the preposition at the end of the clause.

> *Who does this belong to?*   Informal
> *To whom does this belong?*   Formal

Indefinite pronouns

The indefinite pronouns are used when you do not know or do not need to say precisely who or what you are referring to. The noun phrase which they substitute for can refer to a person, a thing, or a group of people or things, in which gender and number are not made clear.

> *Someone will have to tell her that she's failed.*
> *Everybody had a wonderful time.*
> *Anything is better than nothing.*
> *Nothing can make up for this loss.*
> *Some people like that sort of thing. Others don't.*

The indefinite pronouns can be grouped according to meaning, as follows:

A General amounts and quantities: *most, some, none, any, all, both, half, several, enough, many, each.*

> *Many find it impossible to cope.*
> *Congratulations from all at the club.*
> *Judging by the comments, most wanted her to stay on.*
> *Although we lost a lot of stuff in the fire, some was saved.*
> *Enough has been said on this topic to fill a book.*

B Choice or alternatives: *either, neither.*

> *Could you bring me one of those spanners? Either will do.*
> *Neither was keen on a traditional wedding.*

C Undefined singular or multiple persons and things:

someone	*somebody*	*something*
no one	*nobody*	*nothing*
anyone	*anybody*	*anything*
everyone	*everybody*	*everything*

> Note the form of *no one* or, less usually, *no-one*.

- The pronouns in group C that refer to people can cause problems concerning the **number** and **gender** of a following determiner or pronoun. Traditionally, only the use of a following **singular** form was permitted. Common practice uses the plural form *their* and avoids awkward expressions like *his or her*.

    Everybody has **their** ups and downs.
    Has *anybody* finished **their** lunch yet?
    No one in **their** right mind goes on holiday there in January.

Many of these pronouns, especially those in groups A and B, have the same form as determiners. See p. 160.

- The way to tell them apart is to see if the word on its own is used as a subject, an object, or the complement of a verb; if it is, it is a **pronoun**. If, on the other hand, it is used in front of a noun, it is a **determiner**.

    As a pronoun:
    Both were given life sentences.
    Several managed to escape.
    I've found *some*!

    As a determiner:
    Both men were given life sentences.
    Several sheep managed to escape.
    I've found *some scrap paper*.

- The pronouns in Groups A and B are often used like partitives, with *of* and a noun phrase or a personal pronoun.

  > *None of the children were hurt, but most of them were rather upset.*
  > *Neither of his parents remarried.*

Prepositions

A preposition is one of a small but very common group of words that relate different items to each other. Most English prepositions have a number of meanings that are particular to each preposition.

Simple prepositions consist of one word, e.g. *in, on, under.* Complex prepositions consist of more than one word, e.g. *due to, together with, on top of, in spite of, out of.*

Prepositions enable us:

– to express movement to or from a **place**.
– to express **location** and **time**.

Prepositions are normally followed by:

– a noun phrase.

> *in time*   *over the edge*
> *under the table*   *together with my friends*

– an *-ing* clause.

> *Thanks for looking.*
> *He picked up some extra cash by working in a bar at night.*

– a relative pronoun (**WH-** word).

> *He's married to Rachel, with whom he has one daughter.*

In everyday speech a preposition may end a relative clause rather than come before it. See also p. 270.

> *That's the girl we were talking about.*
> *That's the man (who) I gave the money to.*

A preposition needs an object, rather like a transitive verb. A preposition and the noun phrase that goes with it is called a **prepositional phrase**.

A prepositional phrase is used as an **adverbial**.

> *He put the flowers on the table.*
> *She shut the dog in the kitchen.*
> *He found the papers in time for the meeting.*

or a **postmodifier**.

> *The house* **on the corner** *has at last been sold.*
> *The flowers* **on the table** *are from Tim.*
> *A bird* **with brilliant plumage** *roamed the lawns.*

• Prepositions combine with some verbs to make new meanings from the combination. These are one type of **phrasal verb**. See p. 81.

> *I believe in his innocence.*
> *I stand for justice.*
> *She went through a bad patch.*

The list below shows all the common simple prepositions. Some words can be either **prepositions** or **adverbs**, depending on how they are used and what they combine with. The words in *italics* are the prepositions that can also be used as **adverbs**.

> *aboard, about, above, across, after,* against, *along, alongside,* amid, among, *around,* as, at, atop, bar, *before, behind, below, beneath, beside, between, beyond, by,* despite, *down* during, for, from, *in, inside,* into, like, *near,* of, *off, on,* onto, *opposite, outside, over, past,* pending, per, prior, pro, re, regarding, *round, since,* than, *through, throughout,* till, to, towards, *under, underneath,* until, unto, *up,* upon, via, with, *within, without.*

The example below shows adverbial uses.

> He went **in**.
> I took it **through**.

When a verb is followed by a preposition, there is often little or no choice as to which preposition to use, e.g. *rely on, speak to, give to*.

When there is a choice of preposition, the meaning changes with each:

check for, check on, check over; speak to, speak about; talk to, talk with.

Prepositions allow us to express relationships. These are mostly to do with place and time. Some prepositions can be used with more than one meaning, depending on how we think about the time or place we are discussing.

Prepositions of location

Prepositions can indicate:

– the direction in which something is moving in relation to another person or thing: *towards, from, to, off*.

> They ran **towards** the station.
> He took the road **from** the town **to** the nearest village.

– something or someone being enclosed: *within, in, inside, outside*.

> The lake can be seen from most positions **within** the room.
> There seems to be something loose **inside** the control box.
> You have to stand **outside** the room while we make up some
>   questions.
> Did you put the cheese back **in** the fridge?

– being at a certain point: *on, at, by, near*.

> *Don't stand on the beds.*
> *I'll meet you at the library.*
> *There is a huge park near where I live.*

– movement over or onto a place: *over, across, on, onto*.

> *Graham jumped onto the back of the lorry.*
> *He slid the packet across the table.*
> *Warms tears flowed over his cheeks.*

– location as a line: *along, over, on*.

> *We walked along the bank of the river.*
> *Please sign on the dotted line.*

Prepositions of time

Prepositions can also indicate:

– a point in time or a date : *at, on, in*.

> *The baby arrived at 9 pm. on April 1st.*
> *They got married in June.*
> *I'll be with you in five minutes.*

– a period or point of time which marks a change: *before, after, since, until*.

> *We lived there before Mother died.*
> *I went to that school until I was sixteen.*
> *I usually go there after work.*

– the duration of some event: *for*.

> *Helen stayed there for the whole of July.*

Word order in sentences

The order of words in an English sentence is very important. A change in word order often results in a change of meaning.

Many other languages use **inflection**, a change in the form of words, to show how the parts of a sentence function. English has very few inflections, so the place that a word occupies in a sentence, its **syntax**, is the most important feature.

Neutral word order

Most sentences have a subject, and then something that is said about the subject, which is usually the rest of the sentence. This divides the sentence into the **subject** and the **predicate**.

> John (subject) *bought the tickets on Saturday* (predicate).
> The wall (subject) *was torn down* (predicate).
> My elderly mother (subject) *is rather deaf* (predicate).

Most sentences put the information that they carry in this order. This is neutral word order. When this neutral order is changed, the meaning of a sentence also changes.

> *The cat killed the dog.*
> *The dog killed the cat.*
> *The child watched the rabbit.*
> *The rabbit watched the child.*

Word order in simple sentences

Simple sentences are those which have only one clause. They are extremely common in all forms of written and spoken English. Simple sentences have a normal word order which varies according to whether the sentence is:

– a **statement**,

> *I saw you at the theatre on Saturday night.*
> *I didn't see you at the theatre on Saturday night.*

– a **question**,

> *Did I see you at the theatre on Saturday night?*
> *Didn't I see you at the theatre on Saturday night?*

– a **command**.

> *You should buy a ticket now.*
> *You shouldn't buy a ticket yet.*
> *Buy a ticket now.*
> *Don't buy a ticket now.*

Word order also varies according to whether the sentence is **negative** or **positive**.

Focusing

When we want to focus the attention of a reader or a listener on a particular word or phrase, we can use variations on neutral order, such as putting the subject last, splitting the clause into two, or repeating some part of the sentence.

Some variations on the theme of neutral word order.

> *We used to call him 'Fuzzy'.*
> *'Fuzzy', we used to call him.*
> *Didn't we use to call him 'Fuzzy'?*
> *'Fuzzy' was what we used to call him.*
> *It was 'Fuzzy' we used to call him.*

Declarative, interrogative, and imperative statements

Each sentence in English provides some type of information.
For example, a sentence can be a statement, a question, a request,
a command, a denial or a response, etc. In English the choice and
order of the parts of a sentence help us express these meanings.

Most statements and denials are in the **declarative**. An important
feature of declarative sentences is that they have a subject that comes
before the verb.

> Our dog *eats* any old thing.
> Our dog *won't* just *eat* any old thing.
> The dog *has* already *been fed.*
> The dog *hasn't been fed* yet.
> We *have* already *won* several races.
> We *haven't won* any races yet.

Most questions are in the **interrogative**. An important feature of
interrogative sentences is that they normally have a subject that
comes after an auxiliary verb.

> *Does* your dog *eat* any old thing?
> *Has* the dog already *been fed*?
> *Hasn't* the dog *been fed* yet?
> *Have* you *won* any races yet?
> *Haven't* you *won* any races yet?

If the subject does come first it will be a special question word.

> *Who won* the race?
> *Which* team *was* it?

- Exceptionally, we can ask questions using the declarative. We do
  this by using a special tone of voice.

You're telling me he has a new car? I don't believe it.
It's raining again? That makes three days running.

Many commands are in the **imperative**. Commands in the imperative have no word that acts as a subject, though the subject is understood to be *you*. Commands in the imperative can sometimes sound rude or impatient.

Eat up quickly. We have to go!
Leave me alone.
On your marks, get set ... go!

- We can make a **request**, which is a type of command, sound more polite by using the interrogative.

Would you feed the dog, please.
Would you mind shutting the door.
Could I have that now, thank you.

Not all imperative sentences are orders or commands. They can be social expressions.

Have a nice day.
Get well soon.
Help yourselves to coffee.

There is also a **subjunctive** form. This is rarely used in English now. It may be used when you want to talk about an improbable or unlikely situation.

If I were Prime Minister, I'd spend more money on education.

The declarative

The **declarative** is used to make statements. A statement is usually the expression of a fact or of an opinion. Statements can be both positive or negative.

> *Kate is not working after all.*
> *Tim wasn't reading your diary.*
> *Helen wasn't talking about you.*
> *I'm not going on holiday this year.*

Declarative sentences always contain a subject and a following verb phrase.

The normal word order for declarative sentences:

subject + verb phrase

> *Kate is working.*
> *Tim was reading.*
> *Helen stared at me in surprise.*

subject + verb phrase + direct object

> *Ross is writing a letter.*
> *Pam borrowed three library books.*
> *Stephen ordered vegetarian lasagne.*

subject + verb phrase + adverbial

> *Dominic was eating very slowly.*
> *Lyndsey was studying in her room.*
> *Mikhail laughed nervously.*

subject + verb phrase + direct object + adverbial

> *Dominic was eating his lunch very slowly.*
> *Lyndsey had been reading a book in her room.*

Certain verbs must have following objects, e.g. *see, find, prefer, take.*

> *She saw her friend.*
> *He found a camera.*
> *They took a holiday brochure.*

Other verbs need, or can have, both a **direct** and an **indirect** object, e.g. *give, buy, offer.*

> *Laura offered* **me** *another biscuit.*
> *Scott's uncle bought* **him** *a new bike.*

The word order can be either:

subject + verb + indirect object + direct object

> *Kate gave* **the dog** *a bone.*
> *Stuart bought* **Marie** *a birthday present.*

or, with the addition of a word that indicates the recipient:

subject + verb + direct object + *to/for* + indirect object.

> *Kate gave a bone* **to the dog.**
> *Stuart bought a birthday present* **for Marie.**

Another group of verbs must be followed either by an object and an adverbial expression, or an adverbial expression on its own e.g. *put, place, stand*.

> *Richard placed the computer* on the table.
> *Diana put her jeans* in the drawer.
> *Michael stood* in the middle of the pitch.

A further type of declarative statement has the same basic order of subject and verb as the **subject + verb phrase + direct object** example on p. 227, but with a **complement** replacing the direct object. See p. 230 for more about complements and p. 11 for more about objects.

> *Elisabeth seems to have been rather worried lately.*
> *This dessert is delicious.*

Complements

Some verbs such as *be, become, seem,* do not have an object but a
complement.

The **subject complement** is a word or phrase that tells us more about
the subject.

> *Alan is a nice person.*
> *Rajiv is a psychiatric nurse.*
> *Alison seems very well balanced.*
> *Rosamund is herself again.*
> *That's it!*
> *This is for you.*

The subject complement is linked to the subject by a verb, and the
order is as follows:

subject + verb + subject complement

Subject complements may be either noun phrases, pronouns,
adjectives, or even prepositional phrases.

- Most adjectives can be used after a group of verbs that includes:
  appear, be, become, look, seem, smell, taste, etc. An adjective that is
  used in this position is called a **predicative** adjective and it is
  functioning as a **complement**.

  > *The tickets seemed expensive, but the show was excellent.*
  > *These little cakes are delicious.*
  > *Soon afterwards, Patrick became ill.*
  > *Jackie appeared friendly enough when I first met her.*

Less frequently we find an **object complement**. The object complement
tells us more about the direct object. It relates directly to the object
and is placed after it.

Verbs that can take an object complement with their direct object include *make*, *call*, and *appoint*. The word order is as follows:

subject + verb + direct object + object complement

> *Peter's phone call made Maureen* happy.
> *She called me* a fool.
> *They appointed him* Director.

Word order in negative statements

In negative statements, the basic word order for subject and object is the same as in positive statements.

> *John has gone to school.*
> *John has not gone to school.*

The difference is that negative statements must contain *not*, and must have as part of the verb phrase, either:

- a **primary auxiliary** verb,

> *She had not arrived in time for lunch.*
> *Kate is not working this evening.*
> *Tim was not reading your diary.*

- one or other of the **modal auxiliary** verbs, or

> *I warn you, he may not want to come.*
> *Ailsa could not see the road clearly.*

- a form of *be* used as a main verb.

> *That is not my book.*

The word *not* is added immediately after the first one of these auxiliary verbs. The main verb follows.

The word order is, therefore:
 subject + **auxiliary** + *not* + **main verb.**

A negative sentence may contain a modal verb and one or more auxiliaries as well.

I **may** *not* **have** *gone by the time you arrive.*
They **could** *not* **have** *seen her – they were asleep in bed.*
They **should** *not* **have been playing** *in the road.*

In this case the word order is:
subject + modal + *not* **+ primary auxiliary + main verb**.

If the verb phrase does not already contain one of these verbs, then it is necessary to add the **supporting auxiliary** verb *do*.

The present simple and the past simple tenses of main verbs take the appropriate form of *do*, and then add *not* followed by the base form of the main verb.

He runs.
He **does not** *run.*
He ran.
He **did not** *run.*
Lynn **does not** *work overtime now.*
The bus service **did not** *run on Sundays.*

The word order is, therefore:
subject + *do-* **auxiliary +** *not* **+ main verb**

See p. 235 for more on the supporting auxiliary.

• The contracted form of *not*, which is *n't*, can be used after every auxiliary verb except *am*. This is the most common spoken form.

He **doesn't** *run.*
He **didn't** *run.*
Lynn **doesn't** *work on Sundays.*
She **hasn't** *been to work all week.*
He **isn't** *going to come after all.*
Bill went swimming but Ann **didn't** *fancy it.*

The full form with *not* tends to be used more in writing.

> *can + not* is usually written *cannot*.
>
> *She can't come.*
> *She cannot come.*

- Other words with a negative meaning, *never*, *barely*, *hardly*, *scarcely*, *rarely*, do not change the order of words in a statement.

    She doesn't buy Vogue.
    She never buys Vogue.
    He barely earns enough to live on.
    I hardly think that is going to put them off.

The interrogative

The interrogative is normal for many questions. It contains a verb phrase that is followed by a subject.

There are two main types of question: those that can be answered *yes* or *no*, and those that have to be answered with a specific piece of information or a sentence such as *I don't know*. Each type of question has its own special word order.

Yes/no questions

Questions that expect the answer *yes* or *no* are called **yes/no questions** or sometimes, **polar questions**.

The **interrogative** is used to form yes/no questions.

The normal sentence order for the interrogative is:
   modal/auxiliary verb + **subject** + **base form** of the **main verb**.

> *Were the dogs barking?*
> *Have you been dieting?*
> *Can Mahmoud come too?*
> *Must you go so soon?*
> *Would you like a chocolate?*

When a sentence does not contain a modal verb or an auxiliary verb, the question is formed by placing a form of the supporting auxiliary verb *do* before the subject and following it with the **base form** of the main verb.

> *Does he enjoy tennis?*
> *Do they he play a lot?*
> *Did that surprise his mum?*

Yes/no questions also have a negative form. **Negative yes/no questions** are almost always contracted. The negative in its contracted form *n't* comes immediately before the subject.

> *Doesn't he like talking about his childhood?*
> *Can't Peter have one too?*
> *Don't you speak French?*
> *Wouldn't you like to know a bit more about this?*

If the full negative form *not* is used, it comes immediately after the subject. The full form is very formal.

> *Does he **not** like talking about his childhood?*
> *Do you **not** want to know what it was about?*
> *Can Peter **not** have one too?*

WH- questions

When you want to get a detailed answer, not just *yes* or *no*, you must use a **WH- question** (or **'non-polar' question**), which allows for many possible answers. The words *who, whom, whose, what, which, when, where, why,* and *how* are used to form this sort of question. These words are referred to as **WH- words**. See pp. 237–240.

> **Yes/no:**
> *Did you ring the school? – Yes, I did.*
> *Was she all right in the end? – No/I don't know.*
> *Have you seen Ali yet? – Yes, I have.*

> **WH-:**
> *Who was that man? – He's my geography teacher.*
> *What did he say when you told him the news? – He was too surprised to say anything.*
> *When did you see Ali? – Last Wednesday.*
> *Where is Peter going? – To work.*
> *When did they arrive? – Yesterday.*
> *Why have you stopped going running? – The doctor told me to.*

WH- words

The **WH-** words are also called **interrogatives**. They are used for WH- questions. They can be determiners, adverbs, or pronouns.

WH- determiners

When used as determiners, *what*, *which*, or *whose* can be used to ask questions:

– about nouns

> *What book are you reading?*
> *Which plane is he catching?*
> *Whose jacket is this?*

– or about the pronoun *one* or *ones*.

> *Which one would you like?*
> *Which ones did Ruth want?*

• The determiner *which* can be used in questions about selecting. It can also be used together with the preposition *of* for the same purpose.

> *Which colour shall we use?*
> *Which book sells the most copies?*
> *Which of these colours shall we use?*
> *Of all your novels, which of them did you enjoy writing the most?*

• The determiner *whose* asks about possession with reference to a person as the possessor.

> *Whose mother did you say she was?*
> *Whose bag is this?*

WH- adverbs

The adverb **WH-** words, *when, where, how,* and *why,* always make the sentence follow the interrogative word order.

– *When* asks about time.

> *When will they arrive?*
> *When shall I see you again?*

– *Where* asks about place.

> *Where are you going?*
> *Where have you been?*
> *Where is your coat?*

– *How* asks about manner.

> *How did you get here? – We came by train.*
> *How does this thing work?*

– *Why* asks about reasons and purpose. Questions with *why* are usually answered with a clause containing *because* to express reason, or with the *to* infinitive to express purpose.

> *Why is the baby crying? – Because she's hungry.*
> *Why are you saving your money? – To buy a bike.*

– *How much* implies reference to a quantity; *how many* implies reference to an amount or a countable number of things but may leave out the noun referred to.

> *How much money did they take? – All of it.*
> *How much does it cost? – £4.20.*
> *How many packs do you want? – Twelve, please.*
> *How many do you want? – Twelve, please.*

- *How* can also be used with adjectives such as *old*, *big*, *far*, or with adverbs such as *often*, *soon*, *quickly* to ask about degree, rate, or timing.

> *How far is it to the station? – About five kilometres.*
> *How often does he come? – Not very often.*

WH- pronouns

The **pronouns** *who*, *whose*, *which*, and *what* can be the subject or object of a verb.

> *Who can help me?*
> *Whose is the new sports car outside?*
> *Which was your best subject at school?*
> *What happened next?*
> *What have you got to take with you to camp?*

The interrogative pronoun *whose* is used when the question is asked about a person as the possessor of something. See also pp. 201–202 on interrogative and relative pronouns.

> *Whose is the motorbike parked outside?*
> *Whose is this?*

• The form *whom* is used as the object of a verb or of a preposition in very formal or old-fashioned English.

> *Whom did you talk to?*
> *Whom would you rather have as a boss?*

Modern English usage prefers *who* instead of *whom* in all but the most formal contexts.

> *Who did you talk to?*
> *Who would you rather have as a boss?*

When *whom* is used as the object of a preposition, it normally follows the preposition.

> *To whom did you speak?*
> *With whom did she go?*

When *who* is used, the preposition is placed at the end of the clause.

> *Who did you speak to?*
> *Who did she go with?*

The **WH-** subject pronouns are found in the same sentence order as statements:
WH- subject pronoun + the main verb.

> *Who can help me?*
> *Whose is that motorbike parked outside?*
> *Which was your best subject at school?*
> *What happened next?*

The **WH-** object pronouns make the sentence take the word order of a question:
WH- object pronoun + primary or modal auxiliary + subject + base form of the verb.

> *What do you have to take with you to camp?*
> *What has Jonathan done now?*

- The exception to this is in informal spoken English, when the speaker wants to show shock or disbelief.

> *You did what?*

Sentence tags

Tags are short additions that look like questions, used at the end of a declarative sentence. They are sometimes called **question tags**, but many sentences ending with a tag are not real questions. They are usually used to check that the listener agrees with what the speaker has said. Sentence tags are very commonly used in spoken English, but not in formal written English.

The tag is added to the end of a statement. If the auxiliary verb *be* or *have* or a **modal** verb is part of the verb phrase in the sentence, then it is used as the verb in the sentence tag.

> It *isn't* raining again, *is it?*
> You*'ve seen* the programme, *haven't you?*
> Well, we *can't jump* over it, *can we?*
> You *will come, won't you?*

If the main verb is in the present simple or past simple tense, the tag is made using *do*.

> He certainly *likes* eating, *doesn't he?*
> I *slipped up* there, *didn't I?*

In negative tags, *n't* is added to the auxiliary. Note that this contracted form is always used.

> He certainly *likes* eating, *doesn't he?*
> I *slipped up* there, *didn't I?*
> They *went* with you, *didn't they?*

- The formal forms such as, *does he not, did I not, have you not,* sound old-fashioned. They are more common in some regional varieties of English.

The pronoun in the sentence tag must match the subject of the main verb.

> *You aren't listening, are you?*
> *He reads a lot, doesn't he?*

Sentence tags can be **negative**

> *They went with you, didn't they?*

or **positive**.

> *Your father doesn't belong to the golf club, does he?*

Normally, when the first part of the sentence is positive, the tag verb will be negative, and vice versa. Sentences in which both parts are positive are less common. These sentences must be used carefully as, with certain tones of voice, they can sound aggressive or judgemental.

> *I see, you think I'm a fool, do you?*
> *So you smoke now, do you?*

• The same sentence tag may have different meanings depending on the tone of voice that is used with it.

> Falling tone: statement
> *She's gone out, hasn't she?*

> Rising tone: question
> *She's gone out, hasn't she?*

The sentence can be a statement of fact or a question, depending on whether your voice rises or falls at the end. However, a question mark is always required.

Sentence tags are used in the following combinations:

- To say something that the speaker expects the listener will agree with. This doesn't always sound like a question:

positive main verb + negative tag

> *Mary will pass her driving test this time, won't she?*
> *Richard seems to have lost interest in everything, doesn't he?*

or **negative main verb + positive tag**

> *Jessica didn't care, did she?*
> *Kerry hadn't done enough preparation, had she?*

- To point out or remark on something, often something that the listener cannot deny. This frequently sounds more like a question:

positive main verb + negative tag

> *You've just bought a new car, haven't you?*
> *Henry has been away already this year, hasn't he?*

or **negative main verb + positive tag**

> *Desmond hasn't been to see you, has he?*
> *Paula wasn't in your class at school, was she?*

- To show interest in something. This often repeats part of what the previous speaker has said:

positive main verb + positive tag

> *You saw him in town, did you?*
> *So, you come from New Zealand, do you?*
> *So you've just come back from skiing, have you?*

When a tag is used to show interest in something, the sentence is often begun with *So*. This type of tag can also be used in a challenging manner.

> *Oh, so you've been here all the time, have you?*

After a command, a tag made with *can, could, will, shall,* or *would* makes an order more polite.

> *Make me a cup of tea, will you?*
> *Just wait a minute, would you?*
> *Let's go to the cinema, shall we?*

The imperative

Commands and orders

The **imperative** is used to give commands and orders. The form of the verb used for the imperative is the **base form** of the main verb, which is used without a subject.

> *Walk to the corner, turn right, and cross the road.*
> *Open your mouth and say 'Aaaah'.*

- Although the main feature of sentences in the imperative is that they have no **grammatical** subject, they do have an **understood** subject, *'you'*.

The basic form of the imperative remains the same whether it is addressed to one or more people.

> *Come on, Mary; I'm waiting.*
> *Come on, girls; you're late.*

There is also a special type of imperative, using *let's*, that is used when you need to include the speaker. See p. 247.

The word order of a sentence in the imperative is:
verb + **object** (if needed).

The negative imperative is made with *do + not* or *don't*.

> *Don't lose that key.*
> *Do not come back without it!*

The uses of the imperative are as follows:

– to give an order.

> *Go away.*
> *Stop that.*
> *Keep quiet.*

– to give instructions.

> *Don't use this spray near a naked flame.*
> *Apply the glue thinly and leave it for ten minutes.*

– to give advice or warnings.

> *Don't forget to take your passport with you.*
> *Be careful!*
> *Don't go on the ice.*

– to make an offer or an invitation.

> *Have a piece of cake.*
> *Come round and see me some time.*

The imperative of *do* + a **main verb** can be used:

– for polite emphasis.

> *Do take your coat off.*

– to be persuasive.

> *Do try to eat a little of this; it will be good for you.*

– to show irritation.

> *Do stop talking! I'm trying to work.*

• Note that the imperative is not the only way to form a command or an order. You can also issue a command when you use a sentence in the declarative or the interrogative.

> *I'm certainly not going to get it – you get it.*
> *Would you get it, then? I'm busy.*

Making suggestions

Let's (*let* + *us*) + **main verb** is used in the 1st person plural only, especially when you are trying to encourage someone to do something with you.

It includes both the speaker and the hearer, so the subject that is understood is represented by the plural *we*.

> *Let's visit Malcolm this weekend.*
> *Please let's go to the cinema tonight.*
> *Do let's have a look at your new computer, Chris.*
> *Let's pool our resources.*

• Suggestions which start with *let's* often end with the sentence tag *shall we?*

> *Let's phone her now, shall we?*
> *Let's go for a walk after supper, shall we?*

In ordinary English the negative is *let's not* + **main verb** or sometimes *don't let's* + **main verb**.

> *Let's not worry about that now.*
> *Don't let's worry about that now.*

In formal English, the negative is *let us not* + **main verb**.

> *Let us not lose sight of our aims.*

Do let's is the emphatic form.

> *It's a very good bargain; do let's buy it!*

- The uncontracted form *let us* + **main verb** is occasionally used in formal and written English.

> *Let us be clear about this.*
> *Let us hope that this will never happen again.*

The answer to a suggestion with *let's* is normally either, *yes, let's* or *no, let's not* or sometimes, *no, don't let's (...).*

> *Let's phone her now, shall we? – Yes, let's.*
> *Let's phone her now, shall we? – No, let's not.*
> *Let's invite Malcolm over this weekend. – No, don't let's do that.*

The vocative

The imperative is often used with a **vocative**. This is where you mention a person's name or some other way of identifying the person to whom a command or request is being addressed.

> *David, come here!*
> *Come here, David.*
> *Hey, you, stop talking!*

The vocative can be a proper noun, the pronoun *you*, or a noun phrase.
The vocative can come before or after the main clause.
A vocative forms a part of many questions.

> *Peter, do you know where I put the DVD?*
> *Have you seen Chris recently, Jenny?*

A vocative is also combined with an interrogative clause to form a request.

> *Tony, would you pass me the hammer?*
> *Could I speak to you privately for a minute, Sue?*

When a vocative is used with an imperative clause, the sentence is usually a command.

> *Sam, get off there!*
> *You, come back!*

A command can also be phrased as a request.

> *Would you stop talking now, darling, and go to sleep.*
> *Would you get off there, please, Sam.*

A practical reason for using a vocative is to supply the missing but understood subject, so that the right person will understand the command or request, and act on it.

Note the punctuation. There should be a comma between the vocative part of the clause and the remainder.

As part of a command, except for urgent warnings, the use of the vocative is considered rude or abrupt.

The subjunctive

The **subjunctive** was formerly used in English for situations that were improbable or that expressed a wish. It is only rarely used in modern British English. It is, however, found in certain set phrases and in very formal forms of speech and writing.

> God *save* the Queen!
> God *bless* you!
> God *help* us!
> Heaven *help* us!
> Heaven *forbid* that that should happen to me.
> *Suffice* it to say he escaped with only a caution.

The present subjunctive

The form in the present tense is exactly the same as the base form in all persons of the verb. That is, there is no -s on the 3rd person singular.

The subjunctive is used, in very formal English, in subordinate clauses that follow verbs expressing a desire, a demand, a formal recommendation, or a resolve.

> I only ask that he *cease* behaving in this extraordinary manner.
> It is vital that they *be* stopped at once.
> Is it really necessary that she *work* all hours of the day?
> I demand that he *do* something to make up for this.

The clause containing the subjunctive is linked to the main clause with *that*.

- This use of the subjunctive is more common in American English than in British English. British speakers usually take advantage of other ways of expressing the same message, especially in less formal speech.

> *I only ask that **he should cease** behaving in this extraordinary manner.*
> *It is vital that they **are stopped** at once.*
> *It is vital **to stop** them at once.*
> *Is it really necessary **for her to work** all hours of the day?*
> *I demand that **he does** something to make up for this.*

The past subjunctive

In written English and in very formal speech, the past subjunctive form *were* is sometimes used with the 1st and 3rd person singular, in place of the normal past form *was*.

The past subjunctive may be used:

– after *if* or *I wish*, to express regret or longing

> *If your father **were** alive he would help you.*
> *If I **were** rich I would buy a Ferrari.*
> *I wish I **were** taller.*
> *If only he **were** here now!*

– after *as if/as though* and similar expressions, to express doubt or improbability.

> *You talk to him as if he **were** your slave!*
> *Some people behave as though dogs **were** human.*

Many people prefer to use the normal form of the past in this type of sentence. This is quite acceptable in ordinary English.

> *If your father **was** alive he would help you.*
> *If I **was** rich I would buy a Ferrari.*
> *I wish I **was** tall.*
> *If only he **was** here now!*
> *You talk to him as if he **was** your slave!*

Exclamations

Exclamations are short utterances that you make when you are very surprised or upset. They are not always whole sentences. Sometimes they are more like a noise than a word. In this case they are called **interjections**.

> *Ugh!*   *Phew!*
> *Wow!*   *Huh!*

Many exclamations consist of just one word.

> *Help!*   *Nonsense!*
> *Blast!*   *Rubbish!*

Exclamations can also consist of:

– *what* + **noun phrase**

> *What a pity!*
> *What a lovely day!*
> *What rubbish!*

– or *how* + **adjective**.

> *How silly!*
> *How kind of him!*

They may also have the form of a negative question.

> *Isn't it a warm day!*
> *Aren't they kind!*

- Another form of exclamation is when the hearer repeats part of the sentence that he or she has just heard. This is used when the hearer finds it hard to believe what has been said or is very surprised. This sort of exclamation is called an **echo**.

    Richard's passed the exam. – Richard's passed! That's brilliant!
    Sally's here. – She's here! What a relief!

Responses

Responses are made in answer to a question or a statement by another person in the course of conversation. Like exclamations, they may be full sentences, but can also be phrases or single words.

> *Yes.*
> *On Tuesday.*
> *I certainly will.*

Responses usually do not make sense on their own.

Although a response may not have a subject or contain a main verb, it can be classed as a sentence, because a response uses our knowledge of what has just been said. The subject or the verb will usually be understood from the context.

> *Are you coming to the party tonight? –* **Yes.**
> *When are you going to London, then? –* **On Tuesday.**
> *Will you be doing some shopping? –* **I certainly will.**

- If the verb is in a simple tense you can use the supporting auxiliary *do* as the verb in the response.

> *Do you like courgettes? – Yes, I* **do.**

- You usually just use the first part of the verb phrase in a compound verb to make a response. That is, the first **auxiliary** verb or the **modal verb** becomes the response form.

> *Has Tamsin called round yet? – Yes, she* **has.**
> *Was Andrea crying? – Yes, she* **was.**
> *Can we leave early? – Yes, you* **can.**
> *Should I be doing this differently? – Yes, you* **should.**

Some speakers prefer to use the modal and the auxiliary form together.

Laurence could be running if it wasn't for his injury.
  – Yes, he **could be***.*

Sentences and clauses

A clause is a group of words which contains a verb. The verb in a clause can be finite

> *Use this pan for the pasta*
> *He missed the turnoff.*

or non-finite.

> *To cook pasta, always use a large pan.*
> *Dreaming about Jenny, he missed the turnoff.*

Simple sentences

Simple sentences consist of one clause, in which the verb is finite.

> *Ann went to the bank.*
> *She withdrew £100.*

Two or more clauses can be joined to make a **compound** sentence or a **complex** sentence.

Complex sentences

Complex sentences are those that contain a **subordinate** clause as well as a **main** clause.

> *When he arrives, I'll phone you.*
> *He stayed at home because he felt ill.*

A **subordinate** clause is one that contains special information about the main clause. It will usually be introduced by a **linking word** such as *when, if, because,* or *that.* The linking words are called **subordinating conjunctions**.

Most subordinate clauses can come before, after, or within the main clause. Usually, when one clause is of principal importance and the other clause gives information about the principal one, we have a complex sentence with one **main clause** and one **subordinate clause**.

- The position that a subordinate clause is placed in is determined largely by what is felt to be the main message of a sentence.

> *Since you seem to have made up your mind, I'll say no more.*
> *I stopped seeing her because she moved to Liverpool.*

Compound sentences

A compound sentence is one that consists of two **main clauses**, joined by a word such as *and*, *but*, or *or*, called a **coordinating conjunction**. Each clause is of equal importance and gives information of equal value. The order of the clauses can be very important for the meaning. For example, the timing of an action can be described by the order in which the clauses follow each other.

> *He picked it up and ran over to her.*
> *He ran over to her and picked it up.*
> *I drove to Coatbridge and went on to Stirling.*

Compound-complex sentences

These have more than one main clause and at least one subordinate clause.

> *Angie came over and we decided to use my car because hers*
> *was playing up.*
> *He ran over to Julie, who was sitting at the end of the bench,*
> *and grabbed her handbag.*

Joining clauses

Coordination

The process called **coordination** joins two short clauses of equal importance with a conjunction. Each clause becomes a **main** clause in the new sentence.

> *Ann went to the bank and withdrew £100.*
> *Sally goes to work but Ann doesn't have a job.*
> *Ann (either) stays at home or visits her family.*

The clauses are linked by words called **coordinating conjunctions**, such as *and, but, (either) or, neither, nor,* or *yet.* Conjunctions come at the beginning of a clause.

• If the subject of both clauses is the same, it does not have to be repeated in front of the second verb.

> *She came over and ~~she~~ gave me a hug.*

The conjunction *and* is used:

– to join clauses where there is no contrast or choice.

– to join more than two clauses; the earlier clauses can be joined by a comma, but the last two must be joined by *and*.

> *Ann got into the car, drove to the bank, withdrew £100,*
> *and went shopping.*

The conjunction *but* is used to join clauses where there is a contrast.

> *She wanted to buy a new dress but she couldn't find one she liked.*

The conjunction *yet* is used, mainly in written English, to join clauses where there is a contrast that is of a surprising nature.

> *He's a quietly spoken man,* **yet** *he still manages to command attention.*
> *She was suffering from a knee injury* **yet** *she still won the match.*

- The conjunctions *and, but, or, neither,* and *nor* are also used to join two phrases of the same kind,

> *This book is useful for* **planning and carrying out** *research.*
> **The former President and his wife** *were there.*

or two words of the same class.

> *I use this chair when I am* **reading and working.**
> *Do you undertake* **detailed or intricate** *work?*
> **Jack and Jill** *fell down the hill.*
> *This is a* **complicated but intriguing** *film.*

In particular, *and* and *but* are used to coordinate pairs of adjectives in a predicative position.

When there is a positive choice between the subjects of two clauses, you use the pair of words *either* and *or* to join the clauses.

> **Either** *you come to my place* **or** *I'll meet you at work. Which do you prefer?*

If the subject of the joined clauses is the same, the subject is used in the first of the joined clauses only. This is often also true of any auxiliary verbs that may be present.

> *Martin said he would* **either** *meet them for lunch* **or** *take them to tea.*

When it is used in this way *either* must come in one of these places:

- before the subject in the first clause of the group.
- in front of the main verb and after any auxiliary verb.

You can use *either...or* to join more than two clauses if you repeat the use of *or*.

> *Colin said he would (either) meet them for lunch,*
> *(or) take them to tea, or have them over for a coffee.*
> *Ian can (either) come with us or take a taxi later.*

The use of *either...or* emphasizes that the two clauses are alternatives and cannot both be true. Compare *and/or*.

> *Colin said he would meet them for lunch, and/or have them*
> *over for a coffee.*

The word *either* can be left out if the sentence meaning is clear. Some writers treat all but the final *or* as optional.

> You can use *or* on its own to join two or more clauses,
> but *either* cannot be used on its own.

When there is a negative choice between the subjects of two clauses, you can use the pair of words *neither* and *nor* to join the clauses.

> *It is neither possible nor desirable that they should be invited.*
> *Jane was not a fool; neither/nor was she prepared to be blamed*
> *for the error.*

The word *neither* can be used on its own to connect two clauses if the first clause contains a word with broad negative meaning such as *not*, *barely* or *scarcely*. If there is a subject in the second clause, question order must be used.

There was barely enough meat for the children; neither did they have any bread.
Eric hardly saw the fight; nor did he remember much about the incident later.

- The words *either* and *neither* can also be used as a pronoun or as a determiner. Each can then be used on its own; it does not then have a joining function.

  Either book will do. It doesn't matter.
  Neither book is at all suitable, I'm sorry.
  You can have either.

- *Either*, *or*, *neither*, and *nor* can be used as conjunctions inside a noun phrase or a verb phrase.

  You can choose to study either Shakespeare *or* Keats.
  Neither Vimala *nor* Katie *knew the answer.*
  She is either desperate or just silly.
  He didn't know whether to stay or go.

Subordination

When two or more clauses are joined by a conjunction other than *and*, *but*, *or*, or *yet*, one of the clauses is the main clause; the other clauses are **subordinate** clauses. The different types of subordinate clause include **noun** clauses,

> *What matters most is **that you treat everyone fairly**.*

adverbial clauses,

> *They went outside **as soon as the rain stopped**.*

relative clauses,

> *This is the problem **that we're facing** at the moment.*
> *We stayed in Inverness, **which is in the Scottish Highlands**.*

conditional clauses,

> *Maureen plans to live in Australia **if she can get a job there**.*

and **reported** clauses.

> *She told me **that Philip was in France**.*

Each of the subordinate clauses is associated with an introductory word that signals what type of clause it is that follows.

> ***After** she had read the diary, she returned it to the drawer.*
> ***As** they were going downstairs, the phone rang.*
> *They aren't coming **because** they've had an argument.*

These words are called **subordinating conjunctions**. They include:

– the **WH-** words

– words like *since, if, when, because*

– the word *that*, either on its own or used with another word
  e.g. *so that* or *supposing that*

– a phrase ending in *as*, e.g. *as soon as, as long as*

• Each of the subordinating clauses has a preferred position. For example, most adverbial clauses usually follow the main clause, although they can also come before the main clause.

> *Shall I do the shopping **when I finish work**?*
> ***When I finish work**, I could do the shopping for you.*

Reported clauses usually follow directly on from the main reporting clause. See p. 277.

Noun clauses

These are clauses that can be used as either the subject or the object of a sentence or in other places where a noun phrase is usually found. They are introduced by *that*

> *What I like about him is **that he always tries his best**.*

or by a **WH-** word, e.g. *who, when, where*.

> *I don't know **where you live**.*
> ***How the thief got in** is a mystery.*
> ***Why she acts like this** is beyond me.*

Word order after a **WH-** word is the same as in a statement.

> The subordinating conjunction *that* can often be omitted.
>
> *I think that he'll succeed.*
> *I think he'll succeed.*

Adverbial clauses

Adverbial clauses generally follow the main clause unless otherwise stated. The following are the main types of adverbial clause:

Time: sets the timing for the main clause.

> *We should go as soon as you are ready.*
> *I'll call for you whenever you like.*
> *Since she went away, I haven't been able to sleep.*
> *The moment he said it, I started to feel better.*

− may come before or after the main clause.

− introduced by *after, as, as soon as, before, once, since, till, the moment (that), until, whenever, when, while*.

Place: sets where the action of the main clause takes place.

> *I put it where nobody would find it.*
> *He made an impact everywhere that he went.*
> *Wherever you looked, he was to be found.*

− introduced by *where, wherever,* or *everywhere*.

Manner: sets out how the main clause was carried out.

− introduced by *as, as if, as though, how, just as,* or *the way that*.

> *Mandy looked as if she had seen a ghost.*
> *Cameron wandered in, the way that he does.*
> *You have to fasten it as though it was a shoelace.*
> *The room was decorated just as he had imagined.*

Reason: sets out the thinking behind the action of the main clause.

> *I don't want to go because I'm not keen on old movies.*
> *Since no one was ready, I sat down and turned on the TV.*

– may come before or after the main clause.

– introduced by *as*, *because*, or *since*.

Purpose: sets out what it was hoped would be achieved by carrying out the action of the main clause.

> *Put it just there so that it holds the door open.*
> *Leave a bit for Becky in case she's hungry when she gets in.*

– introduced by *so that*, *in order that*, *in case*, or *lest*.

• Purpose can also be indicated by *so as to*, *in order to* followed by the base form of a verb.

> *I'm living with my mum and dad so as to save money.*
> *He put the chair against the door in order to hold it open.*

Result: sets out what happened when the main clause was carried out.

> *Ben was so angry that he kicked the wall hard.*
> *Nina is such a generous person that she's often short of money.*

– introduced by *so* + **adjective/adverb** + *that* or by *such a* + **noun phrase** + *that*.

Contrast: suggests that something else may need to be taken into account regarding the main clause.

> *However much you may want to spend your money, try to*
> *save a little each month.*
> *Although it had rained, the ground was still very dry.*
> *We must try to do something for the environment, even if we*
> *can't solve all the world's problems.*

– may come before or after the main clause.

– introduced by *although, even though, even if, however, much as,* or *while.*

Relative clauses

Relative clauses tell us more about nouns. They function rather like adjectives, and are found as **postmodifiers** in a noun phrase. The noun that is modified is called the **antecedent**. Relative clauses normally begin with *who, whom, whose,* or *that.*

These words are called **relative pronouns**. Note that some of them also function as interrogative pronouns. See also p. 211.

A relative pronoun can be the subject

> *The people who live upstairs are having a party.*
> *The dog that bit me had to be put down.*

or object

> *I don't like the music that they are playing.*
> *A man whom I met on holiday phoned last might.*

of the verb in the relative clause. If it is the object, it can be left out in ordinary informal speech and writing.

> *I don't like the music they are playing.*
> *A man I met on holiday phoned lat night.*

Subject and object relative pronouns come at the beginning of the relative clause.

• A relative pronoun can also be the object of a preposition.

> *It was definitely Diana to whom she was referring.*
> *It's a great game at which anyone can excel.*

In informal English a relative clause can end in a preposition, especially if the relative pronoun is omitted.

> *It was definitely Diana that she was referring to.*
> *It's great game which anyone can excel at.*

Defining and non-defining relative clauses

There are two sorts of relative clause.

Some relative clauses act rather like an adjective by providing more information about a particular noun.

> *The people who live upstairs are having a party.*
> *I don't like the music that they're playing.*
> *The girl who was on the bus with us is called Sonia.*

These are called **defining** relative clauses or **restrictive** relative clauses. A defining relative clause is never separated from the noun by a comma.

The other type of relative clause adds extra information to the whole of the main clause. These are **non-defining relative clauses** or **non-restrictive** relative clauses. This type of clause is separated from the main clause by commas.

> *The man next door, who works from home, kept an eye on the house for us.*
> *Thomas went home early, which was a relief to us all.*
> *We stopped in Dryburgh, which is a good place for a picnic.*

Compare:

Defining.
My brother who lives in Canada is a lawyer.
(There are several brothers. The Canadian one is a lawyer.)

Non-defining.
My brother, who lives in Canada, is a lawyer.
(There is only one brother. He is a lawyer. He happens to
   live in Canada.)

Conditional clauses

Conditional sentences consist of a main clause and a **conditional clause** (sometimes called an *if*-clause). The conditional clause usually begins with *if* or *unless*. The conditional clause can come before or after the main clause.

> *We'll be late if we don't leave now.*
> *We'll be late unless we leave now.*
> *If we don't leave now, we'll be late.*
> *Unless we leave now, we'll be late.*

There are three main types of conditional sentence.

Type 1

The main clause uses *will*, *can*, *may*, or *might* + the **base form** of a main verb. The *if*-**clause** uses the present simple tense.

> *If you take the first bus, you'll get there on time.*
> *She'll be cold if she doesn't wear a coat.*
> *If you need more helpers, I can try and get some time off work.*

Type 1 sentences refer to the future. They suggest that the action in the main clause is quite likely to happen.

> *They will not finish their homework unless they start now.*
> *If you book early, you will get a seat.*

The use of the modal verb *may* or *might* in the main clause suggests that there is some doubt whether the main verb action will be achieved.

> *If you book early, you may get a seat.*
> *Mary might deliver your parcel, if you ask her.*

Type 2

The main clause uses *would*, *could*, or *might* + the **base form** of a main verb. The *if-clause* uses the past simple tense

> *If Jim lent us his car, we could go to the party.*
> *We would save £3.50 a day if we didn't eat any lunch.*
> *If burglars broke into my house, they wouldn't find any money.*
> *Would you be very angry if I failed my exam?*

or the past subjunctive.

> *If I were you, I'd phone her straight away.*

Type 2 sentences refer to an imaginary situation. They imply that the action in the *if-clause* will probably not happen.

> *If I won the lottery, I would buy a house in France.*
> *(...but I don't think I'll win the lottery.)*
> *If you didn't spend all your money on lottery tickets, you could afford a holiday.*
> *(...but you do spend all your money on lottery tickets.)*

The past subjunctive is often used when giving advice to someone, especially about what the person should do.

> *If I were you, I'd tell them the truth.*

Type 3

The main clause uses *would*, *could*, or *might* + *have* + the **past participle** of a main verb. The *if-clause* uses the past perfect tense.

> *We could have had a longer holiday, if we hadn't spent so much money on the house.*
> *If I had known about the exam, I would have paid more attention in class.*

In Type 3 sentences the speaker is looking back from the present to a past time and event. The speaker is talking about what might have happened but did not, either because the wrong thing was done or because nothing was done. This type of sentence is used when making excuses, showing regret, blaming, or giving an explanation.

Conditional clauses can also be used to talk about consequences, or to give an opinion about a situation in the following ways:

– The *if-clause* uses the present simple tense and the main clause uses the present simple tense. This is used to refer to universal truths.

> *If you heat water to 100°C, it boils.*
> *Plants die if they don't get enough water.*

– The *if-clause* uses the present simple tense and the main clause is in the imperative. This is used to give advice or orders for particular situations or sets of circumstances.

> *If the alarm goes off, make your way outside to the car park.*
> *If a red light shows here, switch off the machine.*

– The *if-clause* uses the present continuous or present simple tense and the main clause uses a modal verb. This is used to make suggestions and give advice.

> *If you're thinking of buying a lawnmower, you could try mine first.*
> *You should turn down his radio if you don't want the neighbours to complain.*

– The *if-clause* uses *will/would* and the main clause uses a modal verb.

This is used to make a request or to give a polite order.

> *If you'll wait a minute, the doctor can see you.*
> *If you would sign here, please, I'll be able to send you the books.*

> Note that a *'d* in the main clause is the contracted form of *would*. However, a *'d* in an *if*-clause is the contracted form of *had*.
>
> *I'd have gone if he'd invited me.*
> *I would have gone if he had invited me.*
> *I would've gone if he'd invited me.*

In the main clause the contracted forms of the modals used in speech and informal writing are:

I'd have	or	**I would've**
I could've		**I might've**

Reporting speech

There are two ways of writing down or reporting what was said on any occasion. We can repeat the actual words used (**direct speech**),

> *Monica said, 'There's nothing we can do about it.'*

or we can build the words into our own sentences (**reported speech**).

> *Monica said that there was nothing we could do about it.*

The words reported are normally accompanied by a **reporting verb**.

> *Monica said/declared that there was nothing we could do about it.*
> *'There is nothing we can do about it,' Monica replied.*

Another name for reported speech is **indirect speech**.

Direct speech

Direct speech gives the actual words that the speaker used. It is common in novels and other writing where the actual words of a speaker are quoted.

> *Monica said, 'There's nothing we can do about it.'*

The **reporting verb** may come before the words that were actually spoken, or after them, or at a natural pause inside the reported sentence.

> *Monica said, 'There is a nothing we can do about it.'*
> *'There is nothing we can do about it,' Monica said.*
> *'It's no good,' Monica said, 'we'll just have to ask for help.'*

- The comma comes inside the quotation marks, unless the reporting verb is positioned inside a reported sentence that itself does not require a comma.

  There is', Monica said, 'nothing we can do about it.'

- Typical reporting verbs are: *agree*, *answer*, *ask*, *inquire*, *explain*, *say*, *tell*, and *wonder*.

The subject and the reporting verb are sometimes reversed.

  'There is nothing we can do about it,' said Monica.

The actual words spoken always begin with a capital letter, unless the reporting verb comes within a sentence. They are separated from the reporting verb by a comma, unless they are followed by a question mark or an exclamation.

  'Why did you do it?' she asked.
  'Oh, mind your own business!' he snapped.

- The words spoken are enclosed in inverted commas (single or double quotation marks).

  'Have you been to the new shopping mall yet?' enquired Shona.

  "I've already seen it," John replied.

- Single quotation marks are often used to draw attention to a word that is being mentioned for a particular purpose. (See also p. 296.)

  There is no such word as 'fubber'.
  He called me a 'stubborn old goat'.

Reported speech

Reported speech or **indirect speech** reports something that was said, but does not use the actual words that the speaker uttered.

> *Lynn asked whether Pippa had been to the new shopping mall.*
> *Pippa replied that she hadn't, but she had heard that there*
>   *were some really cool shops there.*

Reported speech always has two clauses. The words that are spoken are put in a **reported clause**. There is also a **main clause** that contains a **reporting verb**. The main clause with the reporting verb usually comes before the **reported clause**.

> *Katie told me that Alison is going to resign.*
> *Peter asked whether Mandy was feeling better.*

The reporting verb in the main clause tells us how the sentence was uttered, e.g. *comment, remark, say, tell.* If the reported clause is a **statement**, the main clause is linked to the reported clause by *that*.

> *Mary said that her favourite actor was Ben Whishaw.*
> *John replied that he preferred Scarlett Johansson.*

If the reported clause asks a question, the main verb will be a question verb e.g. *ask, inquire, wonder, query.* The link between the main clause and the reported clause will be *if* or *whether*.

> *Jamie told Dad (that) he had passed his driving test.*
> *Lucy said Alan had been accepted at drama school.*

• The linking word *that* can be left out after most reporting verbs,

> *Jamie told Dad (that) he had passed his driving test.*
> *Lucy said Alan had been accepted at drama school.*

but the links *if* or *whether* cannot be left out.

> *Miriam asked if she could borrow Leonie's mp3 player.*
> *Evelyn wondered whether the concert would be sold out.*

• Speech in a reported clause is not separated from the reporting verb by a comma, is not enclosed in inverted commas, and does not begin with a capital letter unless it is a proper noun. Reported questions are not followed by question marks.

An alternative position for main clauses that would normally have a linking *that*, is after the reported clause. In this case, the link is left out.

> *Harry Potter was on that night, Mary said.*

> Reported clauses can also be used to express what is in someone's mind as well as what is actually spoken.
>
> > *Evelyn wondered whether the concert would be sold out.*
> > *Charlotte thought that she had better go and see her family.*

Changes in the reported words

When you use reported speech, the words put into the reported clause do not exactly match the words actually spoken.

> *'I'll leave here at 8.30 on Friday.'*
> *She says that she will leave home at 8.30 on Friday.*
> *'I'm looking forward to seeing you.'*
> *She says she's looking forward to seeing us.*

Pronouns and **possessive determiners** have to change in reported speech because of the change of speaker, e.g. *I* may become *she*; *you* may become *us* or *him*.

> *'I believe you.'*
> *She said that she believed us.*

> *'I'm leaving you.'*
> *She said that she was leaving him.*

> *'I've finished.'*
> *She said that she had finished.*

Expressions of place and time may also have to change, e.g. *here* may become *there* or *home*; *Friday* may become *in three days' time*.

> *'I've been here before.'*
> *She said that she had been there before.*

> *'I'll see you on Monday.'*
> *She said that she would see him in three days' time.*

The tense in reported clauses

The verb may also change, e.g. *must* becomes *had to* in reported speech. The most common change is a change of tense.

> *'Hello Jake? It's me, Penny. I've arrived here on time, and I'm*
> *going to take a bus to your place. There's one coming now,*
> *so I'd better run.'*

> *She rang to say that she'd arrived there on time and was going*
> *to take a bus to our place. Then she said that one was*
> *coming at that very moment, so she had to run.*

A reporting verb in the present tense can be used in the main clause when you report on a letter or on a recent conversation, e.g. a telephone conversation.

'Hello, Jake? I've arrived here on time, and I'm going to take a bus to your place.'
Penny has just phoned. She says that she has arrived on time and that she's coming here by bus.

However, it is more common to use a past tense when reporting speech.

The changes of tense may be summarized as follows:

direct speech	reported speech
present simple	past simple
present continuous	past continuous
present perfect	past perfect
present perfect continuous	past perfect continuous
past simple	past perfect or past simple
future	conditional

Questions

Verb tenses in reported questions undergo the same changes as in statements. See p. 279.

'Are you ready?'
He asked (us) if/whether we were ready.

'What time is it?'
He asked what time it was.
'Where has Jim gone?'
He wanted to know where Jim had gone.

> Reporting verbs for questions include *ask, inquire, want to know,* and *wonder.*

Direct **yes/no** questions are linked to the reporting clause by *if* or *whether*. **WH-** question words, e.g. *who, when, where*, are used in both direct and indirect questions.

> *'Are you ready?'*
> He asked (us) if/whether we **were** ready.
>
> *'What time is it?'*
> He asked what time it **was**.
> *'Where has Jim gone?'*
> He wanted to know where Jim **had gone**.

- The word order in a reported question is the same as that of a direct statement. Question order is not used in reported speech, i.e. no part of the verb comes before the subject.

Orders and requests

Orders are reported with *tell* + **object** + *to* **infinitive**.

> *'Stop calling me names!'*
> She **told him to stop** calling her names.

Requests for action are reported with *ask* + **object** + *to* **infinitive**.

> *'Please don't leave your things on the floor.'*
> She asked us **not to leave** our things on the floor.

Requests for objects are reported with *ask for* + **object**.

> *'Can I have the salt, please?'*
> He **asked for the salt**.

- The reporting verb can be used in the passive.

> *'Don't park here, please; it's reserved for the doctors.'*
> I was **told not to park** there.

Suggestions, advice, promises, etc.

A variety of verbs can be used for reporting suggestions and similar types of speech. Some of these are:

– *suggest, insist on* + present participle

> '*Let's go to the zoo.*'
> *He suggested going to the zoo.*

– *advise, invite, warn* + direct object + *not* + *to* infinitive

> '*I wouldn't buy that one, if I were you.*'
> *She advised me not to buy that one.*

– *refuse, threaten* + *to* infinitive

> '*I'm not telling you!*'
> *She refused to tell me.*

– *offer, promise* + *to* infinitive

> '*Don't worry; I'll help you.*'
> *He promised to help me.*

Punctuation

The apostrophe (')

Misusing or omitting the apostrophe is one of the commonest punctuation errors.

Showing possession

The apostrophe (') is used to show that something belongs to someone. It is usually added to the end of a word and followed by an -s.

- -'s is added to the end of singular words.

    a baby's pushchair
    Hannah's book
    a child's cry

- -'s is added to the end of plural words not ending in -s.

    children's games
    women's clothes
    people's lives

- An apostrophe alone (') is added to plural words ending in -s.

    Your grandparents are your parents' parents.
    We're campaigning for workers' rights.
    They've hired a new ladies' fashion guru.

- -'s is added to the end of names and singular words ending in -s.

    James's car
    the octopus's tentacles

— **-'s** is added to the end of certain professions or occupations to indicate workplaces.

> *She's on her way to the doctor's.*
> *James is at the hairdresser's.*

— **-'s** is added to the end of people or their names to indicate that you are talking about their home.

> *I'm going over to Harry's for tea tonight.*
> *I popped round to Mum's this afternoon, but she wasn't in.*

• Note that if the word is a classical Greek name, or a historical building, an apostrophe only is sometimes preferred.

> *Dickens' novels*
> *St Giles' Cathedral*

-'s can also be added to:

— whole phrases

> *My next-door neighbour's dog was barking away like mad.*
> *John and Cath's house was on TV last night.*

— indefinite pronouns such as *somebody* or *anywhere*

> *Is this anybody's pencil case?*
> *It's nobody's fault but mine.*

— *each other*

> *We're getting used to each other's habits.*
> *We kept fogetting each other's names.*

When the possessor is an inanimate object (rather than a living thing), the apostrophe is not used and the word order is changed.

> *the middle of the street* (not *the street's middle*)
> *the front of the house* (not *the house's front*)

To test whether an apostrophe is in the right place, think about who the owner is.

> *the boy's books* [= *the books belonging to the boy*]
> *the boys' books* [= *the books belonging to the boys*]

Note that:

– An apostrophe is *not* used to form possessive pronouns such as *its*, *yours*, or *theirs*.

– An apostrophe is *not* used to form the plurals of words such as *potatoes* or *tomatoes*.

With letters and numbers

An apostrophe is used in front of two figures referring to a year or decade.

> *French students rioted in '68 [short for '1968'].*
> *He worked as a schoolteacher during the '60s and early '90s.*

An apostrophe can be used in plurals of letters and numbers to make them more readable.

> *Mind your p's and q's.*
> *His 2's look a bit like 7's.*
> *She got straight A's in her exams.*

REMEMBER

it's = it is, e.g. *It's a holiday today.*
its = belonging to it, e.g. *The dog was scratching its ear.*

Contracted forms

An apostrophe is used in shortened forms of words to show that one or more letters have been missed out. Contractions are usually shortened forms of auxiliary verbs

be	have
I'm	*I/we/they've (have)*
We/you/they're (are)	*He/she/it/one's (has)*
He/she/it/one's (is)	*I/we/you/he/she/it/one/they'd (had)*

would
I/we/you/he/she/it/one/they'd (would)

or the negative *not*.

not
We/you/they aren't
He/she/it/one isn't
I/we/they haven't
He/she/it/one hasn't

In order to work out what the contracted forms *'s* and *'d* represent, you need to look at what follows it:

– If *'s* is followed by an *-ing* form, it represents the auxiliary *is*.

She's reading a book about the ancient Egyptians.
He's going to Ibiza for his holidays.

- If *'s* is followed by an adjective or a noun phrase, it represents the main verb *is*.

  > *She's nervous about meeting my parents.*
  > *He's brilliant at maths.*

- If *'s* is followed by a past participle, it can represent *is* as it is used in the passive,

  > *He's portrayed by the media as a kindly old grandfather.*
  > *It's often said that rock stars are frustrated actors.*

  or *has* as it is used in the present perfect.

  > *She's broken her wrist.*
  > *It's been ages since we last saw you.*

- If *'s* is followed by *got*, it represents the auxiliary *has*.

  > *She's got two brothers and one sister.*
  > *It's got everything you could want.*

- If *'d* is followed by a past participle, it represents the auxiliary *had*.

  > *I'd raced against him before, but never in a marathon.*
  > *She couldn't believe what she'd done.*

- If *'d* is followed by a base form, it represents the modal auxiliary *would*.

  > *I'd give up now, if I were you.*
  > *When we were kids we'd spend hours out on our bikes.*

- If *'d* is followed by *rather* or *better*, it represents the modal auxiliary *would*.

  > *We'd better go home soon.*
  > *I'd rather not talk about that.*

The comma (,)

The comma marks a short pause between elements in a sentence.

Separating main clauses

Main clauses that are joined together with *and* or *but* do not normally have a comma before the conjunction unless the two clauses have different subjects.

> *You go out of the door and turn immediately left.*
> *It was cold outside, but we decided to go out for a walk anyway.*

Separating subordinate clauses from main clauses

Commas are normally used if the subordinate clause comes before the main clause.

> *If you have any problems, just call me.*
> *Just call me if you have any problems.*

Sometimes a comma is used even when the main clause comes first, if the clauses are particularly long.

> *We should be able to finish the work by the end of the week, if nothing unexpected turns up between now and then.*

Separating relative clauses from main clauses

Commas are used to mark off non-defining relative clauses (see p. 271). This is the type of clause that adds to information about a noun or noun phrase.

> My next-door neighbour, who works from home, is keeping an
>   eye on the house while we're away.
> She moved to Los Angeles, where she was immediately signed
>   as a singer songwriter.

Commas are not required in defining relative clauses (see p. 270), since
these simply postmodify the noun.

> Let's make sure the money goes to the people who need it most.
> The computer (that) I borrowed kept on crashing.

Separating items in a list

Commas are used to separate three or more items in a list or series.

> She got out bread, butter, and jam (but bread and butter).

Note that the comma is often not given before the final *and* or *or*.

> They breed dogs, cats, rabbits and hamsters.
> We did canoeing, climbing and archery.

Separating adjectives

Commas are used between adjectives, whether they come before
the noun (i.e. used attributively) or after a linking verb (i.e. used
predicatively).

> It was a hot, dry and dusty road.
> It's wet, cold and windy outside.

A comma is not usually used before an adjective that is followed by
and.

With adverbials

When an adverbial such as *however, therefore* or *unfortunately* modifies a whole sentence, it is separated from the rest of the sentence by a comma.

> *However, police would not confirm this rumour.*
> *Therefore, I try to avoid using the car as much as possible.*

With question tags and short responses

Commas are used before question tags and after *yes* or *no* in short responses.

> *It's quite cold today, isn't it?*
> *He's up to date with all his injections, isn't he?*
> *Are you the mother of these children? – Yes, I am.*
> *You're Amy Osborne, aren't you? – No, I'm not.*

With vocatives

Commas are used to separate the name of a person or group being addressed from the rest of the sentence.

> *And now, ladies and gentlemen, please raise your glasses in*
> *   a toast to the happy couple.*
> *Come on, Olivia, be reasonable.*
> *Dad, can you come and help me, please?*

With discourse markers

Commas are used to separate discourse markers like *Well* and *Now then* from the rest of the sentence.

> *Well, believe it or not, I actually passed!*
> *Now then, let's see what's on TV tonight.*
> *Actually, I quite enjoyed it.*

In reported speech

Commas are used to follow direct speech (if there is no question or exclamation mark after the quotation), or to show that it comes next.

> *'I don't understand this question,' said Peter.*
> *Peter said, 'I don't understand this question.'*
> *'You're crazy!' Claire exclaimed.*
> *'What do you think you're doing?' Dad bellowed.*

It is also possible to punctuate reported speech of the type *Peter said,* '...' using a colon instead of a comma. This is a particularly common practice in American English.

> *Peter said: 'Dream on.'*

In dates

A comma must be used between the day of the month and the year, when the two numbers are next to each other.

> *March 31, 2011*

Quotation marks (' ') or (" ")

Direct speech

Direct speech gives the actual words that a speaker used. It is common in novels and other writing where the actual words of a speaker are quoted (see p. 278).

The words spoken are enclosed in single or double quotation marks.

> *'Have you been to the new shopping precinct yet?'*
>   *enquired Shona.*

> *"I've already seen it,"* John replied.

- The comma comes inside the quotation marks, unless the reporting verb is positioned inside a reported sentence that itself does not require a comma.

> *There is'*, Monica said, *'nothing we can do about it.'*

Other uses

Single quotation marks are sometimes used:

– to draw attention to a word

> *The word* **'book'** *can be used as a noun or a verb.*

– to indicate an unusual use of a word

> *She pointed out that websites used for internet voting could be 'spoofed'.*

– to suggest that the writer want to be distanced from a word.

> *I don't agree with this 'mercy killing' business.*

• Note that the full stop comes after the quotation marks in such cases.

Capital letters

A capital (or 'upper case') letter is used to mark the beginning of a sentence.

> *When I was 20, I dropped out of university and became a model.*

Capital letters are also used for the first letter in proper nouns. These include:

– people's names

> *Jenny Forbes*   *William Davidson*

– days of the week

> *Wednesday*   *Saturday*

– months of the year

> *August*   *January*

– public holidays

> *Christmas*   *Yom Kippur*

– nationalities

> *Spanish*   *Iraqi*

– languages

> *Swahili*   *Flemish*

- geographical locations

> *Australia*
> *Mount Everest*
>
> *Loch Ness*
> *The Mediterranean Sea*

- company names

> *Dyson*
>
> *Harper Collins*

- religions

> *Islam*
>
> *Buddhism*

Capital letters are also used for the first letter in titles of books, magazines, newspapers, TV shows, films, etc. Where there are several words, a capital letter is usually used for all the main content words in the title (i.e. not the prepositions or the determiners – unless they are the first word in the title).

> *The Times*
> *Twelfth Night*
> *Newsnight*
>
> *Hello!*
> *The Secret Garden*
> *Mamma Mia!*

The full stop (.)

Full stops are used:

– to mark the end of a sentence

> *Let's have some lunch.*
> *I have to catch a bus in ten minutes.*

– to mark the end of a sentence fragment

> *Are you cold? – Yes, a bit.*
> *Do you like this sort of music? Not really.*

– in initials for people's names, although this practice is becoming less frequent

> *J.K. Rowling*   *Iain M. Banks*
> *M.C. Hammer*   *Ronald G. Hardie*

– after abbreviations, although this practice is becoming less frequent.

> *P.S. Do pop in next time you're passing.*
> *She's moved to the I.T. department*
> *R.S.V.P. to Helen Douglas on 01234 676240.*
> *The U.S. government reacted strongly to the accusation.*

When an abbreviation consists of a shortened word such as *Re.* or *Prof.*, a full stop is needed.

> *Re. your suggestion that we shorten the lunch hour, could*
> *we arrange a quick meeting to discuss the various options?*
> *Prof. John Johansson will be speaking on the subject of*
> *'Discourse in the Electronic Age'.*
> *Flight BA 345: dep. 09.44 arr. 11.10.*

When an abbreviation contains the last letter of the shortened word, a full stop is not needed.

> *Dr McDonald* *St Mary's School*
> *41, Douglas Rd* *Universal Pictures (UK) Ltd*

- Note that full stops are not used in many common sets of initials,

  > *Did you see that programme on BBC 4 last night?*
  > *Millions of people now call the NHS Direct helpline each year.*

  or at the end of headlines, headings and titles.

  > *Fear grips global stock markets*
  > *Teaching grammar as a liberating force*
  > *Wuthering Heights*

Remember that a full stop, and not a question mark, is used after an indirect question or a polite request.

> *He asked if the bus had left.*
> *Will you open your books on page 14.*
> *I wonder what's happened.*
> *She asked him where he was going.*

In American English, the full stop is called a period.

The question mark (?)

The question mark marks the end of a question.

> *When will we be arriving?*
> *Why did you do that?*
> *Does any of this matter?*
> *He's certain to be elected, isn't he?*

Question marks are used in direct questions, i.e. when the actual words of a speaker are used. A reported question should end with a full stop.

> *The lady said, 'Where are you going?'*
> *The lady asked where she was going.*

Note that you put a question mark at the end of a question, even if the words in the sentence are not in the normal question order, or some words are omitted. Care is needed here as such a sentence can look, at first sight, like a statement rather than a question.

> *You know he doesn't live here any longer?*

A full stop, rather than a question mark, is used after an indirect question.

> *I'd like to know what you've been doing all this time.*
> *I wonder what's happened.*

A full stop also replaces a question mark at the end of a sentence which looks like a question if, in fact, it is really a polite request.

> *Will you please return the completed forms to me.*
> *Would you please call my brother and ask him to collect my car.*

The exclamation mark (!)

The exclamation mark is used after exclamations and emphatic expressions.

> *I can't believe it!*
> *Oh, no! Look at this mess!*

> The exclamation mark loses its effect if it is overused. It is better to use a full stop after a sentence expressing mild excitement or humour.
>
> > *It was such a beautiful day.*
> > *I felt like a perfect banana.*

The colon (:)

The colon indicates a break between two main clauses which is stronger than a comma but weaker than a full stop.

A colon is used:

– in front of a list

> *I used three colours: green, blue and pink.*
> *Make sure you wear clothes made from natural fibres:*
>   *cotton, silk and wool.*

– in front of an explanation or a reason

> *Nevertheless, the main problem remained: what should*
>   *be done with the two men?*
> *I decided against going away this weekend: the weather*
>   *forecast was dreadful.*

– after introductory headings

> *Cooking time: about five minutes.*
> *Start time: 10 o'clock.*

– in more formal writing, between two main clauses that are connected

> *It made me feel claustrophobic: what, I wonder, would happen*
>   *to someone who was really unable to tolerate being locked*
>   *into such a tiny space?*
> *Be patient: the next book in the series has not yet been*
>   *published.*

– in front of the second part of a book title

> *Farming and wildlife: a study in compromise*
> *Beyond single words: the most frequent collocations in spoken English.*

– to introduce direct speech, especially in American English, or when the quotation is particularly long.

> *He said: 'You owe me three dollars and twenty-five cents.'*
> *The Health Minister said: 'The NHS I.T. programme will mean that patients will get access to more comprehensive information to help them make choices.'*

The semicolon (;)

The semicolon is used to mark a break between two main clauses when there is a balance or a contrast between the clauses.

Compare:

The engine roared into life. The propellers began to turn.
The plane taxied down the runway ready for takeoff.

with:

The engine roared into life; the propellers began to turn;
the plane taxied down the runway ready for takeoff.

A useful test to work out when to use a semicolon is to ask yourself whether the two clauses could be written instead as separate sentences. If the answer is 'yes', then you can use a semicolon.

Note that it is quite acceptable to use a full stop in these cases, but a semicolon is preferable if you wish to convey the sense of a link or continuity between the clauses in your narrative.

I'm not that interested in jazz; I prefer classical music.
He knew everything about me; I had never even heard of him.

A semicolon is also used to separate items in a list, especially if the listed items are phrases or clauses, which may already contain commas.

The holiday was a disaster: the flight was four hours late;
the hotel, which was described as 'luxury', was dirty;
and it rained for the whole fortnight.

Brackets ( )

Brackets (also called **parentheses**) are used to enclose a word or words which can be left out and still leave a meaningful sentence.

> *The wooded area (see map below) is approximately
> 4,000 hectares.*
> *This is a process which Hayek (a writer who came to
> rather different conclusions) also observed.*

Brackets are also used to show alternatives or options.

> *Any student(s) interested in taking part should e-mail me.*
> *A goat should give from three to six pints (1.7 to 3.4 litres)
> of milk a day.*

Note that when the structure of the sentence as a whole demands punctuation after a bracketed section, the punctuation is given *outside* the brackets.

> *I haven't yet spoken to John (I mean John Maple, my boss),
> but I have a meeting with him on Friday.*
> *For lunch we had sandwiches (pastrami on rye and so on),
> salami, coleslaw, fried chicken, and potato salad.*

Punctuation is given before the closing brackets only when it applies to the bracketed section rather than to the sentence as a whole.

> *He's very handsome (positively gorgeous in fact!) and still
> single.*

Square brackets [ ]

Square brackets are used, usually in books and articles, when supplying words that make a quotation clearer or that comment on it, although they were not originally said or written.

> *Mr Runcie concluded: 'The novel is at its strongest when describing the dignity of Cambridge [a slave] and the education of Emily [the daughter of an absentee landlord].'*

The hyphen (-)

The hyphen joins words or parts of words.

Hyphens are used at the ends of lines where a word has been split, to warn the reader that the word continues on the next line. If the word you need to split is clearly made up of two or more smaller words or elements, you should put the hyphen after the first of these parts. Otherwise, you put the hyphen at the end of a syllable.

> *wheel-barrow*   *inter-national*
> *listen-ing*   *compli-mentary*
> *infor-mation*

It is best not to add a hyphen if the word is a short one, or if it would mean writing just one or two letters at the end or beginning of a line. For example, it would be better to write 'unnatural' on the line below, rather than writing 'un-' on one line and 'natural' on the next.

Prefixes that are used in front of a word beginning with a capital letter always have a hyphen after them.

> *a wave of anti-British feeling*
> *a neo-Byzantine cathedral*

A hyphen is used to join two or more words that together form an adjective, where this adjective is used *before* the noun it describes.

> *an up-to-date account*
> *a last-minute rush*
> *a six-year-old boy*

The hyphen is omitted when the adjective so formed comes after the noun or pronoun it describes.

The accounts are up to date.
It was all rather last minute.
He's six years old.

Some common compound nouns are usually written with hyphens.

mother-in-law   *great-grandmother*

Hyphens can be used to split words that have been formed by adding a prefix to another word, especially to avoid an awkward combination of letters or confusion with another word.

re-elect
re-covering furniture
re-creation

The dash (–)

A spaced dash (i.e. with a single space before and after it) is used:

– at the beginning and end of a comment that interrupts the flow of a sentence.

> *Now children – Kenneth, stop that immediately! – open your books on page 20.*

– to separate off extra information.

> *Boots and shoes – all shapes, sizes and colours – tumbled out.*

An unspaced dash (i.e. with no space before or after it) is used:

– to indicate a range.

> *pages 26–42*

– between two adjectives or noun modifiers that indicate that two countries or groups are involved in something or that an individual has two roles or aspects.

> *Swedish–Norwegian relations improved,*
> *the United States–Canada free trade pact*
> *a mathematician–philosopher*

– to indicate that something such as a plane or a train goes between two places.

> *the Anguilla–St Kitts flight*
> *the New York–Montreal train*

The slash (/)

The slash separates letters, words or numbers. It is used to indicate alternatives, ratios and ranges, and in website addresses.

he/she/it
200 km/hr
the 2001/02 accounting year
http://www.abcdefg.com

Punctuation in numbers

Dates

Full stops or slashes are often used in dates.

	American usage
12.3.09	*3/12/09*
2.28.11	*2/28/11*

Scientific usage

Full stops are not used in scientific abbreviations.

12 kg	*50 cm*

Times

Full stops and occasionally colons are used in times.

4.15 p.m	*21.15*
3:30 a.m	*20:30*

Long numbers

Commas are used in numbers to mark off units of thousands and millions.

1,359	*2,543,678*

Decimals

Full stops indicate decimal points.

1.5   25.08